THE VOGUE OF REVOLUTION
IN POOR COUNTRIES

THE VOGUE OF REVOLUTION
IN POOR COUNTRIES

Forrest D. Colburn

PRINCETON UNIVERSITY PRESS   PRINCETON, NEW JERSEY

Library of Congress Cataloging-in-Publication Data

Colburn, Forrest D.
The vogue of revolution in poor countries /
Forrest D. Colburn.
p.   cm.
Includes bibliographical references and index.

ISBN 0-691-03676-4 (CL)
1. Developing countries—Politics and government.   2. Developing
countries—Economic policy.   3. Socialism—Developing countries.
4. Developing countries—Colonial influence.   5. Revolutionaries—
Developing countries.   6. Revolutions—Developing countries.
7. Intellectuals—Developing countries—Political activity.
I. Title.
JF60.C645   1994
320.9172′4—dc20   94-10318

Everything begins in mysticism and ends in politics.
  —*Charles Péguy*

Revolutionaries are the mystics of the twentieth century.
  —*Edmundo Desnoes*

Culture is simultaneously the fruit of a people's history
and a determinant of history.
  —*Amílcar Cabral*

Contents

Preface _____

THIS WORK is a comparative study of the many revolutions that have taken place in the poorer countries of the world during a relatively compressed period of time, from 1945 to 1990. During this epoch, which marked the end of European colonialism, leaders in countries as disparate as mammoth China and tiny Grenada, ancient Iran and newly created Guinea-Bissau, and Catholic Nicaragua and Buddhist Burma attempted to remake their societies radically. What can be concluded about the origins of these revolutions and their outcomes? In formulating some answers, I hope to illuminate and give meaning to the drama of these revolutions, and to elicit appreciation for the many hopes and tragedies they spawned.

My inspiration for this endeavor goes back to reading about Mozambique in the Sandinista newspaper *Barricada*. On those warm evenings in Managua, when I had so little to do, I stretched out the thin newspaper coverage by speculating on the similarities and differences between revolutionary Nicaragua and Mozambique. I cannot say why reading about Mozambique was so thought-provoking, but my interest in comparing contemporary revolutions was stirred, and that interest persists.

I have spent a considerable amount of time living and working in Nicaragua. After an eleven-month residence there in 1981–1982, I returned repeatedly during the rest of the decade, for periods ranging from two weeks to three months to nearly a year (in 1985). From there I made a brief excursion to Cuba in 1982; I returned to that island again in 1987. Most enriching were the six months I spent teaching in Ethiopia at Addis Ababa University during the 1987–1988 academic year. In 1991 I made a hurried trip to Burma and Vietnam. Throughout this period I read avidly the articles and books of scholars who were writing the kind of empirically grounded assessments of other revolutionary regimes that I was writing about Nicaragua. This set of experiences provides the platform from which I try to synthesize an understanding of the many revolutions of our time.

My work in Nicaragua was at the invitation of the Instituto Centroamericano de Administración de Empresas (INCAE), and I am grateful for the support given to me there by Marc Lindenberg and other colleagues. I spent most of 1985 working with the Nicaraguan Ministry of Agricultural Development and Agrarian Reform (MIDINRA) and am appreciative of that opportunity made possible by the then-minister,

Comandante de la Revolución Jaime Wheelock, and for the camaraderie of Beatriz Joya of MIDINRA. Dessalegn Rahmato, at the Institute of Development Research, Addis Ababa University, invited me to Ethiopia, and a Fulbright Lectureship funded my stay. At Princeton University, the Latin American Studies Program provided the opportunity to return repeatedly to Nicaragua. The Center of International Studies at Princeton, under the leadership of Henry Bienen, funded my second visit to Cuba and my travel to Burma and Vietnam. The Peter B. Lewis Fund of the Center of International Studies funded a sabbatical, during which time the book was begun.

Helpful comments on earlier drafts of the work were provided by Paul Berman, Jorge Castañeda, George Downs, Susan Eckstein, Carlos Forment, Lynn Hunt, Michael Jiménez, Elizabeth Kiss, Roy Pateman, Minxin Pei, Ben Schneider, Mark Selden, Kathleen Thelen, Robert C. Tucker, Norman Uphoff, William Wohlforth, and Crawford Young. My greatest intellectual debt is to a group of scholars of the French Revolution who have imaginatively argued for a rehabilitation of the study of revolutionary politics. They include most prominently François Furet, Lynn Hunt, Robert Darnton, and Simon Schama.

THE VOGUE OF REVOLUTION
IN POOR COUNTRIES

1

Introduction, Definitions, and Thesis

THE SINGLE most consequential historical phenomenon is probably the expansion of European political and economic influence throughout the world between 1492 and World War II. European expansion is an easily identifiable sequence of events in world history. Beginning with Columbus's fateful Atlantic crossings, the Americas were colonized and their indigenous populations ruthlessly subjugated. Concurrently, Africa fell prey to the establishment of coastal settlements and trading outposts, culminating in the division of the whole continent among seven European countries between 1880 and 1914. European dominance was never as complete in Asia as in the Americas or Africa, but while little of Asia was "settled," its existing societies were infiltrated economically and controlled politically.

The capability—and sheer audacity—of European states to carry out this expansion is hardly comprehensible. Britain, at the height of its intrusion into Asia, controlled one-fifth of the area of the world and a quarter of the population. Zaire is seventy-seven times the size of Belgium, its colonizer. More astounding, however, were the effects of European colonialism on the rest of the world, especially in the Americas, where whole new societies and states were spawned. In Africa and Asia, societies were shuffled and remade in the colonial image. Economic activity and its organization, language, religion, culture, boundaries and identity, the institutions and customs of government, all were profoundly transformed by colonial imprints. Such societal and cognitive miscegenation took a terrible and unrelenting toll.

Most Latin American nations achieved political independence in the early nineteenth century, even before several major European states, including Germany and Italy, were constituted. Elsewhere, though, European colonialism ended only in the post–World War II era. From the late 1940s to the 1970s, nearly all of Africa and Asia became independent. As a result, membership in the United Nations tripled between 1945 and 1990, rising from 51 to 159.[1] In some cases, independence was freely and charitably granted, while in others it resulted

---

[1] Ben Crow and Alan Thomas, *Third World Atlas* (Milton Keynes, England: Open University, 1983), p. 10.

from protracted negotiations. In still other instances, it was achieved only through bloody warfare.

Independence from European domination took place in a highly charged global setting—the Cold War between the United States and the Soviet Union. The competition between those two powerful states gave rise to shrill debates about the ideal paths to political and economic development. The Cold War contributed to a sense of unity among states in Latin America, the Middle East, Africa, and Asia that was promoted by their (1) shared experience of colonialism, (2) relative poverty vis-à-vis Europe and North America, (3) geographic concentration in the Southern Hemisphere, and (4) economic dependence on Europe and North America. These common characteristics gave rise to labels such as the "Third World," the "South," "less-developed countries" (LDCs), and "nonaligned states." The Cold War thus heightened perceptions of national identity and amplified the importance of political ideas and ideologies.

The Cold War notwithstanding, the nations of Europe and North America enjoyed relative harmony after World War II. Among these affluent countries, national identity and place in the world order seemed relatively settled (true even of Eastern Europe until the eve of 1989). Political violence was rare. Latin America, the Middle East, Africa, and Asia were not as fortunate. There, revolutions and wars were linked to the struggle for independence; they came to play the same painful role in state formation that they had historically played in Europe and North America.

Revolutions have been particularly important in contemporary Latin America, the Middle East, Africa, and Asia. They have often been the catalysts for the wars that have plagued poor countries. Moreover, while the impact of wars was largely restricted to the demarcation of boundaries, revolutions—like their earlier European counterparts—have been instrumental in defining national identity, state structures, state-society relations, social stratification, and modes of economic development.

In the poor countries of China, Vietnam, Bolivia, Algeria, Cuba, Cambodia, Ethiopia, Guinea-Bissau, Angola, Mozambique, Burma, South Yemen, Grenada, Iran, Nicaragua, and Afghanistan, revolutions have been consequential for a number of reasons. Domestically, they have spurred debate about how best to "modernize," and they often have been the cause of unparalleled human suffering, witness Cambodia and Ethiopia. They have often been accompanied by devastating wars or counterrevolutions, such as those in Iran, Angola, and Mozambique. Internationally, revolutions have frequently inspired— or instigated—conflict in neighboring nations, as happened with Vietnam and Nicaragua. Revolutionary nation states—Vietnam and Afghanistan, for example—often became embroiled in struggles with either the United States or the Soviet Union, or contributed to conflict between these two great powers, most dramatically illustrated by the Cuban missile crisis. As was true of the French Revolution in the eighteenth century, contemporary revolutions are a major source of international passion, anxiety, and conflict.

The many revolutions of our era have evoked an outpouring of focused studies of revolution in individual countries, cataloging the local and international consequences of radical change. What has not yet emerged is a comprehensive set of generalizations that fits the material across all cases, and into which new material can be fitted. While we do not, for the most part, lack basic data on recent revolutions, we lack explanations—principles by which to classify cases, depictions of intentions and outcomes, and an understanding of patterns of domestic and international conflict—that will hold cross-culturally. There is, in the main, sufficient knowledge, but insufficient understanding.

This work is a comparative analysis of contemporary revolutions in Latin America, the Middle East, Africa, and Asia. I aspire to answer two broad questions:

1. What was the impetus for revolution in such poor countries, and how did revolutionaries believe they had the wherewithal to remake their societies?

2. What explains the largely disappointing, and at times tragic, outcomes of contemporary revolutionary regimes?

In the course of worrying through these two questions, I hope to illuminate the dynamics of modern revolutions and to purchase the underlying proposition of the study: that there are remarkable parallels among revolutions in countries otherwise extraordinarily different from one another.

The central argument of the study is that prevailing interpretations of revolutions have slighted the importance of ideas to which revolutionary elites of our era have been beholden, and the ability of those elites to change the course of history. While the origins of contemporary revolutions are rooted in social, political, and economic conflict, the outcomes of these revolutions have been determined by the political imagination of revolutionary elites, an imagination that came to be surprisingly similar throughout the poorer regions of the world. This fashionable political imagination profoundly shaped the institutional and policy choices of revolutionary elites. Ironically, in an epoch marked by the demise of European colonialism, the minds of those committed to radical change in the poorer countries of the world were

captured by a foreign *mentalité* imported after either immediate or cir-
cuitous exposure to the European socialist tradition. The ensuing pursuit of an idealized state and society proved most problematic.

Definitions and Universe of Cases

The noun "revolution" and its adjective "revolutionary" connote a
varied set of changes. But the purest meaning of revolution is the sud-
den, violent, and drastic substitution of one group governing a territorial political entity for another group formerly excluded from the government, *and* an ensuing assault on state and society for the purpose of
radically transforming society. Political and social change necessarily
coincide. The substitution of one political elite by another may be preceded by years of rebellion, but because the act of revolution is abrupt,
it appears immediate and dramatic. The violent replacement of governors, with all its attendant symbolism, gives a birthdate to the revolution. But it is in the ensuing revamping of society, indelibly slower but
usually violent, too, that the character and the consequences of the revolution are defined.

Without the concerted effort to remake society, an insurrection remains no more than an unconstitutional transfer of power. And no
social elite will transform society, and shift its place in that society,
unless goaded to violently by a usurping elite. Thus, not all insurrections result in revolutions, but it is inconceivable that a dramatic social
transformation is not ushered in by a swift and drastic replacement of
government.

The defining linkage in revolutions between displacing and destroying an old order and trying to rebuild something new suggests that
revolutions should be conceived not as mechanical changes of political
regime or as the necessary conclusions of class conflict, but instead as
the ultimate moments of political choice made only indirectly at most
by the populace. Revolutionary choices are made by a small, self-confi-
dent, maybe politically intoxicated, elite. At the moment power
changes hands, the givens of social existence seem suspended, and
revolutionaries' political imagination suggests that the world can be
made anew. A vision of how things could be different may or may not
be necessary for toppling a governing elite. It certainly helps. However, once power has shifted, a vision that will direct choices—vague,
incomplete, and utopian as it may be—is required for the transformation of society. This vision gives revolutions a logic and dynamic of
their own, one not derivable from the necessity of social conditions or
the ineluctability of social structures and processes.

The comparative study of revolutions in Europe and North America never yielded a consensus on which nations had undergone a revolution. Crane Brinton's masterful and influential study, *The Anatomy of Revolution*, for example, included the United States and England with France and Russia.[2] About the French and Russian revolutions there is no quarrel, but debate continues as to whether the United States and England ever had a revolution. The American War of Independence resulted in a change of government, but it was not accompanied by massive social upheaval. And what some call the English Revolution, others call the English Civil War.

Turning to the post–World War II epoch, there are similar difficulties. There are a few widely agreed upon cases of revolution, but there are also many doubts about how inclusive the term revolution should be. A number of issues are unresolved. Does it matter if governments fall from a war or a military coup d'état, instead of from a popular insurrection? In the aftermath of a violent change of government, if there was an attempt at social transformation, does it matter if the efforts were successful? And the most vexing questions: Just what constitutes "social transformation"? How much of it equates a revolution?

It can be reasonably argued that it does not matter how, or even why, governors are violently replaced. In contrast, what is done with the power seized is consequential. An attempt at social transformation entails a massive, and inescapably violent, restructuring of social stratification. Wealth, income, privilege, opportunity, and status are redistributed. Revolutions attempt to revamp all strata of society, not just to improve the welfare of a certain stratum or to attack the munificence of another. There are no ready and agreed-upon indicators, though, which measure social transformation. And there is no threshold at which it can be decided whether or not sufficient transformation has taken place, or been attempted, for a political upheaval to be judged a revolution. Thus, the designation of what is and what is not a revolution is, in the end, somewhat arbitrary.

Table 1 presents a list of twenty-two countries that I judge to have had a revolution since World War II; they each had a violent change of government followed by an assault on established political and economic orders by new and determined political elites. The degree of social transformation attained varies, but in all cases there was a radical and violent attempt to remake society. A more restrictive definition of social transformation might have excluded such cases as Benin's, while a more inclusive definition might have included cases in still other countries, such as Chile under Salvador Allende's tenure. None-

---

[2] Crane Brinton, *The Anatomy of Revolution* (New York: W. W. Norton, 1938).

TABLE 1
Contemporary Revolutions
Cases and Data 1990

Country	Year	Population (Millions)	Per Capita Income (U.S.$)
Afghanistan	1978	14	160
Algeria	1962	21	2,350
Angola	1975	8	670
Benin	1972	4	290
Bolivia	1952	6	510
Burkina Faso	1983	7	210
Burma	1962	36	180
Cambodia	1975	6	130*
China	1949	1,035	290
Cuba	1959	10	1,400
Egypt	1952	50	700
Ethiopia	1974	40	140
Grenada	1979	.1	1,340*
Guinea-Bissau	1974	.1	160*
Iran	1979	44	2,500
Laos	1975	4	160
Madagascar	1975	10	290
Mozambique	1975	13	120
Nicaragua	1979	3	920
North Korea	1948	20	620
South Yemen	1967	2	510
Vietnam	1945	60	150

*GNP per capita
Source: World Bank

theless, even with these admitted ambiguities of measurement, the list of cases in Table 1 is impressive. Revolution was clearly an important—and widespread—political phenomenon in the poor countries of the world between 1945 and 1990.

In addition to the countries listed in Table 1, many regimes in other countries during the same period of time have claimed to be revolutionary. Their incumbent leaders adopted revolutionary phraseology and implemented policies said to be revolutionary, especially nationalization. Peru and Libya provide two of many good examples. In Peru from 1968 to 1975, the regime of General Juan Velasco instituted sweeping changes under the Plan of the Revolutionary Government of the Armed Forces. The aim was "social proprietorship," in which virtually all enterprises—industrial, commercial, and agricultural—

would be either state- or worker owned and would be managed collectively. Colonel Moammar Qadhafi and other military officers seized control of Libya in 1969 and governed in the name of the Revolutionary Command Council. Reforms that followed included limitations on savings and the consolidation of private shops ("nests of exploitation") into large state supermarkets. While I do not gauge these changes to be deep enough to be truly revolutionary, they do attest to the prevailing fashion of revolution.

The importance of revolution in poor countries during this period is further illustrated by other countries where political life was disrupted, and in some cases irrevocably altered, by the rise of political organizations attempting to instigate revolution. An example is the impact of the Tupamaros on Uruguay; the urban guerrillas never succeeded in sparking a revolution, but their violence contributed to the country's slide into a repressive military dictatorship. Similarly, the Indonesian Communist Party altered politics in that archipelago.

The number of revolutions in countries similar in their poverty and international status, yet geographically and culturally diverse, presents a puzzle worthy of explanation. The puzzle is all the more engaging because these revolutions inspired so many potent political actors in other poor countries.

Thesis

Comparative studies of contemporary revolutions are few. No coherent theoretical explanation of these revolutions has emerged. Most studies of individual revolutions have been grounded in theoretical precepts suggested by the comparative study of revolutions in Europe and North America. The two major interpretive schools, modernization and Marxism, share a preoccupation with the long-term origins and outcomes of revolution. And in explaining both origins and outcomes, discourse and explanation center on impersonal social structures. Modernization and Marxist analyses alike deny the importance of who the revolutionaries were or what they thought they were doing. As a result, political innovations by revolutionaries seem to be either predetermined or accidental, and their consequences seem to be irrelevant.

Unlike Marxism, modernization theory does not have a canonical text. Most of the influential social theorists of the nineteenth and twentieth centuries, including Max Weber, took modernization of some self-defined kind to be the most salient and continuous feature of social life. In most modernization theory, revolution is defined almost tautologically as the characteristic modernizing event. Revolution derives its significance from its contribution to long-term social and political outcomes. The actual experience of revolution is essentially a corrective to lagging social and political adjustments and a painful learning process of trial and (mostly) error. The French Revolution thus facilitated the transition from Louis XVI to Napoleon to elected government.[3]

Perhaps the most influential example of a modernization view of revolution is Samuel Huntington's *Political Order in Changing Societies*. Huntington defines political modernization as having three steps: the rationalization of authority; the differentiation of new political functions and the development of specialized structures to perform those functions; and the increased participation in politics by social groups throughout society.[4] His analysis of revolution grows out of his conception of modernization: "Revolution is . . . an aspect of modernization. . . . [I]t is most likely to occur in societies which have experienced some social and economic development and where the processes of political modernization and political development have lagged behind the processes of social and economic change."[5] The long-term outcome of revolution appears clear and inescapable: restored harmony between "social and economic change" and "political development." The character of the particular revolution is of only passing interest. After all, why should revolutionary politics be of concern if the outcome of the revolution is all but inevitable? There is a disturbing lockstep character to modernization theory's explanations.

In Marxism, revolution plays the same pivotal role: it is the means by which societies lurch *forward*. Karl Marx himself penned the metaphor, "Revolutions are the locomotives of history." Marx explained revolution by the appearance of a new "mode of production" that emerges and grows in the fallows of the reigning mode of production. It ultimately causes social and political conflicts that tear apart the foundation of society. Another regime emerges from the remnants, one that is better suited to the new economy. Modes of production are linked to specific class configurations, so economic competition and change provoke class conflict. The death of a mode of production means the death of a class; the birth of a mode of production means either the birth or the ascendancy of another class.

---

[3] Lynn Hunt, *Politics, Culture, and Class in the French Revolution* (Berkeley: University of California Press, 1984), pp. 7, 208–209.

[4] Ibid., pp. 208–209.

[5] Samuel Huntington, *Political Order in Changing Societies* (New Haven: Yale University Press, 1968), p. 265.

Marx was passionately interested in the French Revolution. He traced its origins to the aggressive self-assertion of the bourgeoisie in the face of aristocratic reaction in the 1780s. For Marx, the revolution had two inseparable results: it fostered the development of capitalism by breaking the stranglehold of feudalism on production, and it brought the bourgeoisie, as a class, to power. Students of Marx have challenged the actual role played by the bourgeoisie and have suggested that other classes, particularly the aristocrats and the peasantry, had more of a role than Marx appreciated. But while there have been many variations to Marx's interpretation of the French Revolution by his students, what remains unchallenged is the extent to which the revolutionary experience is a plastic period between its long-term origins and its outcomes.

Knowledge of the vanguard role of the Bolsheviks in the Russian Revolution, and of the acrimonious debates among such Bolshevik leaders as Lenin, Bukharin, and Trotsky, has not dented the methodological rigidity of contemporary Marxists. They have ignored the argument that Lenin's own role in the Russian Revolution suffices to falsify the claims of "historical materialism."[6] Overwhelmingly, Marxists have clung to their faith in using impersonal economic and social structures to explain the origins and outcomes of revolution.[7]

Despite differences in diction and unspoken but noticeable normative differences, modernization and Marxist theorists are thus alike in attributing radical political change either to the disruption caused by economic growth or to the demands of economic competition. Revolution is conceptualized as the painful readjustment of a society's political and social institutions to the requirements of its expanding economic capacities. The experience is essentially endogenous and progressive. Both schools of thought incorporate revolution into more general causal explanations of historical development in which economic and social structures have priority.

These similarities can be observed in the work of two influential scholars, Barrington Moore and his student, Theda Skocpol. Both combine elements of modernization and Marxism in their cross-national studies of revolution. In his celebrated *Social Origins of Dictatorship and Democracy*, Moore turns Huntington's formulation on its head and argues that "sick societies are ones in which revolutions are impossible."[8] For Moore, revolutions were essential to the establishment of

---

[6] An early and forceful presentation of this argument is given in Sidney Hook, *The Hero in History* (New York: John Day, 1943), pp. 200–228.

[7] Hunt, *Politics, Culture, and Class in the French Revolution*, pp. 3–6.

[8] Barrington Moore, Jr., *Social Origins of Dictatorship and Democracy* (Boston: Beacon Press, 1966), pp. 457–458.

capitalist democracy, whereas failed revolutions, or revolutions from above, led to fascism. Yet despite their conflicting interpretations of the place of revolutions in the making of nation-states, Huntington and Moore are alike in having little interest in—and ascribing little explanatory weight to—revolutionaries and revolutionary discourse and politics. They believe that revolutionaries get swept into their assigned places by inanimate social forces which act like giant brooms.

Skocpol broadens Moore's analysis by highlighting the importance of the international system. There is, she argues, not only class competition and conflict, but also nation-state rivalry, competition, and war. She adds a twist to Marxist analysis by suggesting that the long-term outcome of revolution is not just progression to a more "efficient" economy and the political ascension of a formerly subordinate class; the state itself comes to have growing power and autonomy. Thus, for Skocpol, states figure prominently in both the cause and outcome of revolution. Her study is titled, most appropriately, *States and Social Revolutions*.[9]

The novelty of Skocpol's conclusion obscures its loyalty to the methodological canons to which it is heir. In her introduction, she argues that "social revolutions should be analyzed from a structural perspective."[10] The revolutionaries themselves are overlooked: "Any valid explanation of revolution depends upon the analyst's 'rising above' the viewpoints of participants."[11] Explanation is instead sought in macrostructural and macrohistorical contexts. Skocpol thus continues the ingrained tradition of perceiving politics as resting on a social base or substructure: the character of politics is explained by society; changes in political relationships are traced to prior changes in social relations.

Like its forerunners, Skocpol's interpretation is not so much wrong as it is limited in analytical precision. Her adherence to structural explanation leads her to deprecate, to an implausible degree, the causal significance of political agency. The resulting deduction of politics from social structure is too mechanistic, ignoring the reality that revolutionary politics do not merely follow from social structural preconditions. Politics can, at least at certain moments, sculpt society. And it is precisely during a revolution that politics is most likely to alter society. Through their language, images, and daily political activity, revolutionaries strive to reconfigure society and social relations. They consciously seek to break with the past and to establish a new nation-state. In the process, they create new social relations and, often, novel ways of practicing politics.

[9] Theda Skocpol, *States and Social Revolutions* (Cambridge: Cambridge University Press, 1979).

[10] Ibid., p. 5.

[11] Ibid., p. 18.

I do not mean to suggest that the impetus for revolutions is only intellectual or that politics has invariable primacy over society. A revolution is an explosive interaction between ideas and reality, between intention and circumstance, between political activity and social context.[12] My contention is that there is a tense mutuality between revolutionaries and the societies that created them; neither one can be deduced from the other. Economic history does not determine political history.

It is easy to appreciate the appeal of structural analyses of revolutions in the attempt to understand the political evolution and dynamics of the poor countries of the world. Skocpol's suggestion of the importance of interstate relations is especially persuasive. The machinations of foreign states have played a decisive part in the history of the world's poor countries, most of which are small and weak. It was the poor countries of the world that were the victims—as they were often the outright creations—of imperialism. And there can be no question that colonialism set the stage for many contemporary revolutions. The self-destructiveness of World War II weakened, and in some cases ended, European domination. Given the course of the war, it is not surprising that in its aftermath there was social upheaval in Korea, China, Vietnam, and Burma. And if Churchill had remained in power, India, too, would likely have been torn by even more political upheaval, with democracy an unlikely outcome. In Africa, the reluctance of the French to leave Algeria contributed to that country's radicalization, a lesson ignored by the Portuguese in Guinea-Bissau, Mozambique, and Angola. In these and other cases, Skocpol insightfully suggests that the causes of revolutions be sought in the "specific interrelations of class and state structures and the complex interplay over time of domestic and international developments."[13] The case-study method of Moore and Skocpol ensures, in contrast to more abstract treatments of revolution, that the critical importance of specific historical circumstances is not overlooked.

Yet it is important to acknowledge that the participants make the crucial difference between a potentially revolutionary situation and an actual revolution. Once the revolution is under way, their thinking and behavior influence the revolutionary process. In turn, the course of the revolution, its ebbs and turns, inescapably shapes the outcome.

What is strikingly similar about the twenty-two cases of contemporary revolutions listed in Table 1 is not their structural origins, but the common values and the shared behavior of their leaders—the revolutionaries themselves. The settings were diverse, the roads to power

---

[12] Hunt, *Politics, Culture, and Class in the French Revolution*, p. 13.
[13] Skocpol, *States and Social Revolutions*, p. xiii.

varied, but successful revolutionaries, once in control of the government, proved to have had remarkably similar ideas about how to remake their societies. The values, expectations, phraseology, iconography, and implicit rules that expressed and shaped collective intentions and behavior can be called the intellectual culture of the revolution. And it has been this intellectual culture, I will argue, much more than the imperatives of social structure, that has provided the logic of contemporary revolutions.

The shared intellectual culture of contemporary revolutions has centered on a commitment to "socialism." Despite differences in how that term is conceptualized and articulated, a professed faith in its ideals has led to shared iconography, institutional structures, and economic-development strategies. The most important shared traits are general ones: authoritarian government and a state-led strategy of economic development. But it is notable how universal are some specific features that have resulted from parallel political decisions, features such as neighborhood defense committees and an emphasis on agricultural cooperatives. Since socialism, as an ideology, could not be expected to lead single-handedly to similar institutional designs in so many different settings, it is clear that what has been shared, or copied, is not just the political philosophy of socialism, but a range of characteristics associated with socialist states. Indeed, the one apparent exception, Iran, proves to have much in common with other revolutionary regimes openly embracing socialism.

Paradoxically, the commitment of many revolutionaries to socialism originated more in the teachings and writings of dissident intellectuals in Western Europe and North America than from the examples of such socialist states as the Soviet Union. Once in power, triumphant revolutionaries did copy certain features of established socialist regimes, and assistance from the socialist countries was often crucial to their survival as they struggled to consolidate power, transform their societies, and defend themselves from the inevitable counterrevolution. Still it is intriguing, although ultimately explicable, how much of the political imagination of revolution came from countries that officially disdained socialism, how little was learned by revolutionaries from the actual experience with socialism in the Soviet Union and elsewhere, and how little originality revolutionaries demonstrated. Perhaps the final and ironic legacy of colonialism was thus to provide an alternative conception of state and society, a rejoinder to the one bequeathed by colonialists.

The intellectual culture of contemporary revolutions has permeated revolutionary politics throughout the world. It has informed a myriad of political choices. And in so doing, it has decisively affected national identity, the institutions of government, the scope of government authority, nongovernmental institutions, social structures and social stratification, the distribution of opportunities and resources, and international relations. The impact of revolutionary politics is such that the welfare of every conceivable social grouping, from individuals to the polity at large, has been altered. An appreciation for the import of revolutionary politics can be gleaned from comparing revolutionary countries with neighboring countries with which they share many basic characteristics: for example, Cuba and Jamaica, Mozambique and Botswana, Vietnam and Thailand. Everyday life is never the same.

The intrusiveness of contemporary revolutionary politics is neither accidental nor inherent. The intellectual culture that has informed revolutionary politics in the post–World War II epoch—the political imagination of socialism—is expansive and ambitious. It is possible to imagine other revolutionary political cultures that would be less embracing. Revolutionary intellectual cultures are a flotsam of symbols, impressions, images, ideas, and visions. They are dynamic. They vary temporally and spatially. Perhaps the two most remarkable characteristics of contemporary revolutions are, first, the extent to which they have shared a common intellectual culture, and, second, just how ambitious that intellectual culture has been, especially given the material poverty of the respective polities.

An illustrative parallel can be drawn between the recent attraction of socialism in poor countries and the liberalism with which rebellious European intellectuals in the late eighteenth century fought the hierarchical structures, communitarian customs, and aristocratic ideals of their day.[14] Liberal reformers belittled prevailing political institutions and practices, and concurrently produced an attractive alternative that ultimately reshaped the North Atlantic community of nations. It was another epoch during which ideas mattered.

The power of revolutionary politics calls into question the longstanding theoretical emphasis on structural variables in discussions of revolution. I do not deny that inanimate structural forces help explain the origins of revolutions. Indeed, the evidence presented here largely corroborates the view that revolutions are rooted in profound—if diverse—social, political, and economic crises. The many contemporary revolutions show, however, that there is little necessary linkage between structural origins and outcomes. As Daniel Mornet said of the French Revolution, "The origins of the Revolution are one story, the history of the Revolution is another."[15]

[14] Joyce Appleby, *Liberalism and Republicanism in the Historical Imagination* (Cambridge: Harvard University Press, 1992), p. 7.

[15] Quoted in Roger Chartier, *The Cultural Origins of the French Revolution*, trans. Lydia Cochrane (Durham: Duke University Press, 1991), p. 8.

Naked structural interpretations of revolution are suspect. They need to be complemented by the study of what can at least in certain epochs be a decisive intervening variable—revolutionary intellectual culture. It is advisable to fathom the origins of this culture, its content, and its impact. The study of revolutionary politics needs to be rehabilitated.

Inanimate social forces such as class conflict, markets, and international rivalries are of unappreciated importance as challenges to the feasibility of revolutionary initiatives. These tests represent a major part of the story of contemporary revolutions. Revolutionary elites have attempted a sweeping transformation of society to fulfill their utopian vision of how society should be remade. The implementation of those initiatives has tested the practicality and viability of the dominant revolutionary political culture. There have been some successes, but for the most part, the results have been disappointing, even disastrous. But the point here is not to pass judgment; it is to emphasize that because efforts to remake society were everywhere so ambitious, and were tackled with such zeal, polities have been altered irrevocably. The goals of this generation's revolutionaries have been elusive, but their scope and exhaustive pursuit drained their citizens materially and emotionally. No one, and no place, was the same after the experience.

Both modernization and Marxist theories of revolution suggest that revolutions lead to progress: society lurches forward, even if at great cost. Yet the trajectory of contemporary revolutions challenges this facile conclusion. The nation-states that have undergone revolution look anything but more "modern" for the experience: there does not seem to be any natural progression to a more "efficient" economy; no subordinate class has risen to command effectively the helm of state and society; there is no necessary acceleration of "state-building." Indeed, just the reverse has often occurred. Those countries that have recently gone through the calamities of a revolution seem "backward." Their collective experience has wrought savage and cumulative damage on the rationalist promise of revolution.

As the body politic of the nation-states listed in Table 1 struggled with the unfolding of their revolutionary initiatives and with the reactions they elicited, the intellectual culture that has dominated revolutions since the end of World War II, and that reached its apogee in the 1960s, has withered at a remarkable rate. It began to die where it had originated—in Western Europe and North America. The beginning of the end was probably the wave of revisionist interpretations of the Soviet Union by Parisian intellectuals in the 1970s. The mounting misfortunes of revolutionary regimes, including the sanguinary horrors of Cambodia, sped the decline of revolutionary political culture. The decisive end came with the Soviet leadership's admission of profound doubts about socialism, and the collapse in 1989 of the erstwhile socialist regimes of Eastern Europe. The subsequent demise of the Soviet Union itself precluded any reversal of conviction.

The withering of such an influential revolutionary intellectual culture is an enormously important event. It lessens the likelihood of future revolutions, since revolutions depend not only on structural preconditions but also on actors committed to radical change. Yet there need be no end to radicalism. A new revolutionary political culture may emerge, one that may prove more capable of fulfilling its promises. We are as far as ever from living in a world in which the immediate appeals of revolution have become unintelligible or even in which they have become irrelevant.[16]

Organization

The study is organized around the generalizable political sequence of revolutions. As different as revolutions may be from one another, there are common political events that occur in succession, even if they differ temporally. There are the political crises of and challenges to the *ancien régime*, the insurrection itself, the seizing and consolidation of power by triumphant revolutionaries, the launching of efforts to transform society, and finally the prosaic administration and defense of the state apparatus and its fledgling social initiatives. Organizing the work around these stages, rather than around narratives of individual cases, permits more penetrating comparisons. A good-faith effort is made to draw evenly on the entire set of cases throughout the book, and not to shrink from comparisons that offer contrasting inferences.

Chapter 2 seeks to support the first part of the book's argument by tracing out the development of a common revolutionary intellectual culture throughout the regions of the world colonized by Europe. This endeavor leads to an analysis of the relationship of emergent revolutionaries to dissident intellectuals in Western Europe and North America. These intellectuals were consistently frustrated in Berlin, Paris, London, Lisbon, New York, and Berkeley, but unbeknownst to them, they came to influence profoundly the course of politics in distant societies they had never even visited.

The third chapter explores the interaction of structural variables, intellectual culture, and human agency in explaining the occurrence—

[16] John Dunn, *Modern Revolutions*, 2d ed. (Cambridge: Cambridge University Press, 1989), p. xxvi.

and configuration—of contemporary revolutions. Chapter 4 details the extent to which shared political visions have shaped revolutionaries' agendas for transforming their societies. It examines uniformities in how power is consolidated by triumphant revolutionaries. The design and establishment of new political institutions is outlined, including the relative influence of ideas, of advice and aid from socialist countries, and of political imperatives.

Chapter 5 explores how triumphant revolutionaries' economic agenda has been tested by the exigencies of high expectations, the international economy, the limited managerial abilities of the revolutionary state, and the quest for social acceptance. The tale is one of many proud marches to folly. A brief subsequent chapter outlines the all too frequent bloody challenges that revolutions have provoked.

The penultimate chapter describes the withering of the faith in radical change, and in how it has nearly everywhere been defined as socialism. Again, analysis necessarily returns to the sway of Europe and North America. Finally, Chapter 8 explores some conceptual and theoretical issues raised by the methodology and conclusions of the study.

Cautions

The attempt to compare and contrast the multiple experiences of such a complex political phenomenon as revolution in so many and in such disparate countries poses certain obstacles. First, much remains unknown, secreted away in bureaucrats' desks or buried in the memory of fearful (or dead) individuals. But even the available information about the cases of revolution included here is problematic. Quantitative data, while the most easily comparable, are scanty and often unreliable. Other kinds of information are often dubious as well, as seen from the frequently conflicting accounts of reputed facts and pristine interpretations of even mundane events. There are also the problems of using analytical constructs, such as authority and class, across cultures. It is simply not possible to be as intimate with my subject as I would like. This inevitable shortcoming means, more so than usual, that what is offered cannot be the "truth" in any absolute sense, but merely an interpretation. I do not pretend, either, to have the "right" interpretation, only one that I hope is insightful and useful.

The interpretation offered of contemporary revolutions is neither parsimonious nor possessing an exacting specificity. No neat typology of revolutions is advanced, nor is the course of revolutions found to be governed by inexorable laws of behavior. On the contrary, every effort is made to acknowledge what is unique to particular cases and to stress the importance of historical legacies, individual personalities, and even fate in shaping political outcomes. In arguing that images, ideas, and visions have been important in contemporary revolutions, and that they have been shared by revolutionaries, I recognize that the diffusion of ideas is not a simple infiltration. Reception always entails appropriation, which transforms, reformulates, and exceeds what is received. The circulation of thoughts and cultural models is always a dynamic and creative process.

With these cautions noted, I offer a frame of reference for contemporary revolutions that suggests and explains the similarities and differences among revolutions. Concomitantly, I aspire to reframe our sense of what is characteristic of revolutions, and what is problematic about them.

2

The Intellectual Culture
of Contemporary Revolutions

An Ethiopian scholar, Dessalegn Rahmato, with whom I had corresponded intermittently, suggested I spend my sabbatical for the 1987–1988 academic year in Ethiopia. He said I could teach for a semester in the Department of Political Science and International Relations at Addis Ababa University. I used his letter to secure a Fulbright Lecturer Fellowship, worth a plane ticket and a stipend. Normally a Fulbright Fellowship is judged to be a prestigious award, but not in this case: there had been no program in the social sciences in Ethiopia since the 1974 revolution. I was the only applicant for a program that at the time did not exist.

Addis Ababa University was a pleasant surprise. The university, founded only in 1950, has nine campuses, five in Addis Ababa. I was at the largest and main campus, home of the humanities, the social sciences, the law school, and the administration. The campus is beautiful, situated in one of Emperor Haile Selassie's palaces. An attempted coup in 1960 by the Imperial Bodyguard resulted in the death at the emperor's palace of many of his aides and ministers. The emperor was away in Brazil at the time and survived, but after seeing blood on the walls of the Green Room, where his captive court had been raked by machine-gun fire, he declared, "I will not live here any longer." He moved to another of his palaces and gave the tarnished one to growing Addis Ababa University.

Buildings have been added to the walled campus, but there remain scores of tall cyprus and eucalyptus trees. Amidst them are flowering gardens guarded by haughty stone lions. The bellowing of real lions could sometimes be faintly heard from the nearby Lion Zoo. Tranquillity of the buildings and grounds of the campus is ensured by keeping out beggars and peddlers.

Thus, I had a comfortable base for exploring Ethiopia and researching its vexatious politics. But the university itself offered a fascinating window into the country's revolution. I learned a great deal just within its walls because the university revealed the origins of many of the revolutionary regime's most consequential choices.

From its inception, Addis Ababa University's benefactor had been the United States, in one form or another. The university began as a Jesuit college (where a course was offered on "Proof of the Existence of God"). The Jesuits gave way to the Mormons; in 1961 a University of Utah survey team organized the graduation of the college into Haile Selassie I University, a name that survived until the revolution. The organization and administration of the newly chartered university were modeled after American universities. English was the language of instruction, facilitating the recruitment of American professors—who came in droves. At one point, every faculty member of the law school except the dean was American. And, of course, the United States gave dollars. A crowning, and enduring, contribution to Addis Ababa University was the John F. Kennedy Library, funded by the United States Agency for International Development. The cornerstone was laid by Robert Kennedy in 1966. In the foyer stands a bust of President Kennedy, with his emblazed quotation, "Ask not what your country can do for you. . . . But what together we can do for the freedom of man."

Brighter graduates were sent off to graduate training in the United States and, to a lesser extent, Western Europe, where they encountered superb universities, an embarrassment of riches, racism, and rampant capitalism. In the tumultuous 1960s and early 1970s, the years of the civil rights movement and of student rebellion, many Ethiopian students abroad became radicalized. The same happened at Addis Ababa University, less perhaps because of events in North America and Europe than because of dissatisfaction with the backwardness of Ethiopia and the perceived slowness of its modernization, as well as the mounting struggle against colonialism and capitalism elsewhere in Africa. Still, the ideological currents prominent in North American and Western European universities were also felt at Addis Ababa University.

Both Haile Selassie and his American patrons indirectly contributed to the radicalization by inviting unsuspected "outside agitators" to the university. The emperor established the Haile Selassie African Scholarships for students from English-speaking Africa who had been spurned by British universities. The first group that arrived asked, "Where is the union?" Finding none, they organized one. They did not stop there. Peace Corps volunteers, too, while often dismissed as agents of imperialism, contributed to the radicalization of Ethiopian students.

By the early 1970s Addis Ababa University was intensely politicized. According to one professor, himself a student at the time, "In those days, not to be a Marxist was considered heretical. Students who were only interested in having a good time were dismissed as 'Jolly

Jacks.'" Students, even those in science and engineering, were passionate about learning world history and wondered aloud what it suggested for Ethiopia. There were continuing debates, which attracted crowds of students, on the wide steps outside the language building. When one of the debaters had to run off to class, another student would step in—and the debate would continue. Students gathered together to read the words of Marx, Lenin, Mao, and other revolutionaries. They also organized themselves into a host of student organizations. These organizations periodically held noisy demonstrations, which sometimes moved out of the university and degenerated into riots. Students were often arrested during or after each ruckus, but Haile Selassie would always pardon them.

By early 1974 discontent with the regime had become widespread and was openly expressed, even in the military. Dissatisfaction was heightened by the government's indifference to a famine in 1972–1973. There was a pronounced desire for accelerated economic development and broader political participation. But the emperor, nearing eighty-two years of age, seemed increasingly unable even to manage the reins of government. Finally, on the eve of the Ethiopian New Year in September 1974, a group of military officers bundled Haile Selassie into a Volkswagen and drove him from palace to imprisonment. Many sectors of Ethiopian society viewed the relatively good-natured revolution with caution, but the university community was jubilant. Ethiopian intellectuals abroad hurried home to press for, and participate in, "the construction of socialism."

Returning intellectuals and the university community thought that they should play a dominant role in the revolutionary government, and that soldiers should step aside. And they said so vociferously. During the first anniversary of the revolution, parading students (and others) shouted such slogans as "Down with the Military." Fervent opinions, pronouncements, and proclamations on the desired course of the revolution were issued by students and faculty. From the beginning, the military junta—later known by the newly coined word, the Derg—was wary of the academic community. But many of the socialist measures advanced by the academic community were adopted, either because the soldiers were persuaded by the merits of the measures, or because they had no ideas of their own, or because they were attempting to undercut the claims of the academic community. Also, as one professor put it, "The rhetoric of socialism has much currency that appeals to the masses."

While the academic community prodded—and sometimes protested against—the military, debates over tactics and goals among student-based organizations became acrimonious. The two most important organizations, the Ethiopian People's Revolutionary Party and the All Ethiopian Socialist Movement, became bitter enemies. There were assassinations that led to more assassinations. In January 1977, a demonstration on campus led to competition between the two groups for control of the podium. Guns were pulled and shooting began. No one is sure how many students were killed.

Concurrently, the larger and more militant Ethiopian People's Revolutionary Party began to use terrorism against targets within the military regime, which was increasingly demonstrating that it had no intention of sharing power, even with those likewise committed to its "Ethiopian Socialism." The military government responded ferociously, beginning what came to be known as the Red Terror. Hundreds of students and others who opposed the military, or who simply engaged in "commotion," were killed. Their bodies were dumped in the streets to intimidate the populace. Sometimes parents could not reclaim the bodies of their slain children until they paid for the bullets used to kill them. Thousands were arrested and held for years without charges or a trial. The terror brought calm by the end of 1977, but it left many scars.

Thirteen years after the Ethiopian Revolution, and ten years after the Red Terror, the Derg dissolved itself, and the Provisional Military Government of Socialist Ethiopia gave way to the People's Democratic Republic of Ethiopia. Leadership of the country passed from Major Mengistu Haile-Mariam to Comrade Mengistu Haile-Mariam, general secretary of the Central Committee of the Workers' Party of Ethiopia, president of the People's Democratic Republic of Ethiopia, and commander-in-chief of the Revolutionary Armed Forces.

Many factors, including assistance from the Soviet Union, may be seen as precipitating the Ethiopian Revolution and the institutionalization of the new regime. But it is difficult to escape the conclusion that intellectuals defined what the revolution would entail. Their ideas of Marxism and socialism, appropriated by others, became the foundation of efforts to build a new state, a new society, and a new economy. Intellectuals played a decisive role because of the weakness—or outright absence—of representative institutions. The absence of political parties, vigorous media, outspoken unions, and other institutions of civil society created a vacuum that highlighted the views and political activity of young intellectuals and students.

A ranking Ethiopian military officer who served in the revolutionary government testified to the impact of students and the intellectual culture of Western universities that they appropriated. Dawit Wolde Giorgis defected from the government in 1986 and wrote his memoirs the following year:

In 1969 the army allowed me, with the rank of captain, to enroll in Haile Selassie I University, where I received my first exposure to radical political views.... I never participated as a member of the student movement.... Nevertheless, I learned a lot from the movement, and my ideas about reform began to change.... The role played in the Revolution by Ethiopian students in the United States and Europe has never been fully appreciated. For years the intellectual elite of Ethiopia had gone to study abroad. The 1960s and early 1970s were times of intense political activity among these expatriate students.... The Ethiopian movements abroad were strong and well-organized, surpassed only by the Iranians.... The members of the radical movements saw socialism, especially Marxism, as the only possible redeemer of the oppressed people of Ethiopia.... The Russian, Cuban, and Chinese revolutions were the most widely discussed and admired.[1]

Whatever was learned about existing socialist regimes, such as the Soviet Union, was learned through the filter of North American and Western European writings, in part because of language differences and in part because socialist regimes remained largely closed to the outside world.

In the first revolutions of the post–World War II period, including the Chinese and Cuban revolutions, the sources and manners of diffusion of revolutionary ideology are less transparent. But they include some parallels with the Ethiopian case. The most important similarity is the shared use of Marxism-Leninism to inform the choices of the revolutionary leadership. Also shared is the heightened role of intellectuals and students, seemingly the common result of a number of complementary factors: (1) the weakness of representative institutions in poor countries; (2) the mushrooming growth of universities in the aftermath of World War II; (3) the increased ease by which information, ideas, and trends were diffused throughout the world; and (4) the attractiveness of Marxism-Leninism itself to explain poverty in the context of an era where the wealth of Europe and North America was equated with colonialism and an alternative was posed by the Soviet Union.

In 1949, Mao Zedong became the titular and effective ruler of a united China, the most populous country in the world. From an early age he had been studious and politically active. In 1920 he was forced to flee to Beijing because of his political activities in his native province of Hunan. While in Beijing he purchased many books on communism, three of which are said to have had a profound influence on his thinking: *The Communist Manifesto*, *Class War* by Kautsky, and a book

---

[1] Dawit Wolde Giorgis, *Red Tears* (Trenton, N.J.: Red Sea Press, 1989), pp. 9–10.

entitled *History of Socialism*.[2] In the summer of 1920, Mao said, "On theoretical aspects and, to a certain extent, in practice, I am already a Marxist."[3] And his imagination is said to have been fired by the victory of the Russian Revolution.

Mao's biographers emphasize the disparate influences on the development of his political thinking and his pragmatism.[4] Still, it does appear that Marxism-Leninism had widespread currency among young educated Chinese.

> Traditional ideology was abandoned during the famous New Culture Movement of the 1910s and 1920s, and thoughtful young Chinese sought new doctrines to fill the resulting intellectual vacuum. . . . [T]wo new main ideas emerged as the chief inspiration for the young in China: Western, especially European, nationalism, and Russian Marxism-Leninism, and both soon found representation in political movements that vied for the allegiance of the Chinese people. . . . Gradually . . . the Communists realized that the fusion of the patriotic sentiment of nationalism and the reforming zeal of Marxism-Leninism would broaden their ideological appeal. Increasingly throughout the 1930s and 1940s, the union of these two ideological currents came to be symbolized by a single Communist leader—Mao Zedong.[5]

The Soviet Union, through the Comintern, did provide important assistance to the Chinese Communist Party. This aid, though consequential, does not explain either the ascendancy of Marxism-Leninism or the organizational success of the Chinese Communist Party.

The fortunes of the Chinese Communist Party were tied to the weakening of the Nationalist government by the eight years of Japan's invasion of China (which left most Chinese in Japanese-occupied territory), and by the inept military and economic policies of the beleaguered Nationalists. The disorder and despair in China between 1937 and 1949 may have inflamed political theorizing, but they did not suggest or dictate the contours of political imagination:

> The twentieth century . . . brought into China the tremendous stimulus of foreign thought. Mere disorder as in previous interregnums in China had

[2] Austin Shu, *On Mao Tse-Tung* (Asian Studies Center, Michigan State University, East Lansing, 1972), p. vi.

[3] Ibid.

[4] For example, Stuart Schram, ed., *Mao Zedong* (Hong Kong: Chinese University Press, 1983); and Brantly Womack, *The Foundation of Mao Zedong's Political Thought 1917–1935* (Honolulu: University Press of Hawaii, 1982).

[5] Raymond Wylie, *The Emergence of Maoism* (Stanford: Stanford University Press, 1980), pp. 2–3.

not necessarily produced innovation. The interregnum between the central power of the Ch'ing dynasty to 1911 and the central power established by the CCP [Chinese Communist Party] in 1949 was the period of maximum susceptibility and response to foreign theories of social order.[6]

The ultimate triumph of these "foreign theories" depended on the patient efforts of party leaders to forge a coalition with everyday Chinese, including the peasant majority.

Ho Chi Minh was the founder of the Indochina Communist Party (in 1930) and its successor, the Viet-Minh (1941), and president from 1945 to 1969 of the Democratic Republic of Vietnam. As the leader of the Vietnamese nationalist movement for nearly three decades, Ho was one of the most influential revolutionary leaders of this century. Yet his intellectual formation took place largely in France. Ho left Vietnam on a French merchant ship at the age of nineteen.[7] He was a seaman for three years, then lived in London for two years. He moved to France in 1917, where he remained for six years. Ho became an active socialist, joining the French Socialist Party and adhering to the majority group that split off in 1920 to form the French Communist Party.

After his years of militant activity in France, Ho went to Moscow at the end of 1923. He was inspired by the success of the Communist revolution in Russia and Lenin's anti-imperialist doctrine. Following the death of Lenin, he published a moving farewell to the founder of the Soviet Union in *Pravda*. In 1924 Ho went to Canton, a Communist stronghold, where he began organizing the Vietnamese nationalist movement among exiled Vietnamese. Ho was not to return to Vietnam until 1941—three decades after he had left.

Ho's colleague and gifted military commander General Vo Nguyen Giap described his own intellectual formation in Vietnam during an interview conducted in 1990.[8] Giap studied in Hue at a prestigious academy, where he and other students met secretly to discuss anticolonial articles, particularly those by a "mysterious expatriate"—Ho Chi Minh. His political thinking crystallized when he was hired to assist a Vietnamese teacher who owned an illicit collection of Marx's works in French:

> I spent my nights reading them, and my eyes opened. Marxism promised revolution, the happiness of mankind. It echoed the appeals of Ho Chi Minh, who had written that downtrodden peoples should join the proletar-

[6] John Fairbank, *The Great Chinese Revolution* (New York: Harper & Row, 1986), p. 287.

[7] This summary of Ho Chi Minh's life is drawn from George Kahin and John Lewis, *The United States in Vietnam* (New York: Dell Publishing, 1967), pp. 11–16.

[8] Stanley Karnow, "Giap Remembers," *New York Times Magazine*, 24 June 1990: 22–23, 36, 39, 57, 59–60, 62.

iat of all countries to gain their liberation. Nationalism made me a Marxist, as it did so many Vietnamese intellectuals and students. Marxism also seemed to me to coincide with the ideals of our ancient society, when the emperor and his subjects lived in harmony. It was a utopian dream.[9]

As Giap suggests, it was intellectuals and students who took the lead in organizing and giving political direction to an anticolonial movement that would culminate in revolution.

As in the Chinese and Vietnamese revolutions, the Cuban Revolution had a dominant protagonist. Like Mao, Fidel Castro was active in student politics. He received his political education at the University of Havana.

The themes that Castro repeated in preparing the Moncada [army barrack] assault and in the Sierra Maestra, and which, indeed, have been central to the political education of revolutionary cadres and of soldiers and officers in the FAR [Revolutionary Armed Forces], are evident in his student days.[10]

[T]he University of Havana was a particularly fecund training ground for revolutionaries, in the 1920s and 1930s as well as in the 1940s and 1950s. The students of the 1930 generation, so instrumental in overthrowing Machado and pressing for radical reforms, left activism and radical social ideas as a legacy for those to come.[11]

Castro joined various student organizations and study groups, and participated in demonstrations. In 1948 he read Marx's *Capital* and, in 1949, Lenin's *State and Revolution* and *Imperialism*.[12]

Castro read widely, including the work of the great Cuban poet and nationalist, José Martí. As a leader of the insurrection against the dictator Fulgencio Batista, Castro either did not have or did not divulge an ideology. One of Castro's comrades wrote in his memoirs that in the immediate aftermath of victory, "as far as ideology was concerned, nothing was clear, and Fidel was the greatest enigma of all."[13] Not until two years later, in 1961, did Castro announce that he was a Marxist.

An inconclusive debate has long raged over whether Castro hid his Marxism-Leninism until 1961 for tactical reasons, or whether a potential "social-democrat" was driven to Marxism-Leninism by the politi-

---

[9] Ibid., p. 39.

[10] C. Fred Judson, *Cuba and the Revolutionary Myth* (Boulder, Colo.: Westview Press, 1984), p. 31.

[11] Ibid., p. 25.

[12] Ibid., p. 30.

[13] Carlos Franqui, *Family Portrait with Fidel*, trans. Alfred MacAdam (London: Jonathan Cape, 1980), p. 22.

cal opposition to the Cuban Revolution. That debate, though, obscures how ideas of socialism at the University of Havana and elsewhere in Cuba helped inspire the revolution and how, once formally adopted as the ideology of the Cuban Revolution, they played a decisive role in defining the Cuban Revolution.

The linkage between intellectual trends and revolutions is more apparent in the numerous revolutions that took place in the 1960s and 1970s. Not surprisingly, the successes of the Chinese, Vietnamese, Algerian, and Cuban revolutions inspired intellectuals in other poor countries, especially those still suffering from European colonialism. Ironically, though, information about the uprisings—nearly all of it at a high level of generality—was dispersed throughout the poorer parts of the world largely through material published in North America or Western Europe.

In Portugal's African colonies, Guinea-Bissau, Mozambique, and Angola, wars of liberation led to revolution. Portuguese intransigence precluded a negotiated settlement for independence of the three territories. But the handful of intellectuals who planned and directed the insurrections early on merged aspirations of independence with revolution. Their political formation took place in the "metropolis"—Lisbon. An account of the education of Eduardo Mondlane, the leader of Mozambique's Front for the Liberation of Mozambique (FRELIMO) is revealing:

> [T]he colonial regime in 1950 sent Mondlane to Portugal to continue his education. There he encountered other militant African students trying to forge a coherent anticolonial ideology out of Pan-African, Pan-Negro, Marxist, and antifascist philosophies. Among his cohorts were Amílcar Cabral and Agostinho Neto, who subsequently led the liberation struggles in Guinea-Bissau and Angola respectively. . . . In the face of intensified police surveillance, Mondlane fled Portugal and continued his education in the United States.[14]

Many of the African students in Lisbon were politically active. Amílcar Cabral participated in campaigns for peace and opposition to nuclear power. Others became affiliated with the clandestine Portuguese Communist Party.[15]

Once the insurrections began, military strategies were adopted from China, Vietnam, and Algeria. Samora Machel, who became the politi-

---

[14] Allen Isaacman and Barbara Isaacman, *Mozambique* (Boulder, Colo.: Westview Press, 1983), p. 81.

[15] Ronald Chilcote, *Amílcar Cabral* (Boulder, Colo.: Lynne Rienner, 1991), p. 8.

cal-military leader of FRELIMO after the assassination of Mondlane, is reported to have carefully studied General Giap's theory of "people's war."[16] Success was facilitated by the provision of weapons by the Soviet Union and Eastern European countries.[17] Neighboring African countries provided important logistic support: in Guinea-Bissau, the African Party for the Independence of Guinea and Cape Verde (PAIGC) depended on assistance from Guinea, the People's Movement for the Liberation of Angola (MPLA) received help from Zambia, and FRELIMO had assistance from Zambia and Tanzania.[18] The fighting itself was carried out largely by poor, illiterate workers and peasants; still, the conception of how to obtain independence and remake society in the aftermath of independence came from contact with Portuguese intellectuals and Communists in Lisbon.

A similar relationship emerged in Cambodia, which had been established as a French protectorate in 1863. The revolution that swept through Cambodia between 1975 and the beginning of 1979 was the fiercest and most consuming in this century of revolutions.

> Under the regime of Democratic Kampuchea [the short-lived name given to Cambodia], a million Cambodians . . . died from warfare, starvation, overwork, misdiagnosed diseases, and executions. Most of these deaths, however, were never intended by DK. Instead, one Cambodian in eight fell victim to the government's utopian program of total and rapid social transformation, which its leaders had expected would succeed at far less cost.[19]

These leaders developed their utopian vision for Cambodia in Paris. In the 1950s a generation of Cambodian students in France, including Saloth Sar (who later adopted the name Pol Pot), entered the French Communist Party and envisaged radical solutions to Cambodia's underdevelopment.

> Most Cambodian students in France saw themselves as intellectuals. It was a small step for them to see themselves as a vanguard, ahead and above the rest of their compatriots. Most of them encountered communism and socialist ideas in the heady days between the triumph of communism in China and the death of Stalin four years later.[20]

[16] Barry Munslow, ed.; Michael Wolfers, trans., *Samora Machel* (London: Zed Books, 1985), p. viii.

[17] Rosemary Galli and Jocelyn Jones, *Guinea-Bissau* (London: Frances Pinter, 1987), p. 57.

[18] Basil Davidson, *The Liberation of Guiné* (Harmondsworth, Middlesex, England: Penguin, 1969), p. 117.

[19] David Chandler, *The Tragedy of Cambodian History* (New Haven: Yale University Press, 1991), p. 1.

[20] Ibid., p. 52.

Students reportedly read the works of Marx, Lenin, and Stalin in French; discussions were held in a mixture of Cambodian and French, in part because many political terms had no Khmer equivalents.[21]

In the Middle East, Marxism-Leninism also had a resonance, and it was often in the universities that Marxism-Leninism flourished and found adherents. Ties with European intellectuals, publishing houses, and universities were important. But whereas in other parts of the world overrun by colonialism Marxism-Leninism was the only potent intellectual form of dissent, in the Middle East, and in Afghanistan and Indonesia, there was also Islam.

Islam has a history of centuries, and one not just as a religion but as a force that challenged Western European civilization and imperialism. Despite its divisions, it has both legitimacy and a strong organizational presence throughout the Middle East. Revolutions in the region during the post–World War II period have been characterized—and shaped—by an ideological clash between Islam and distinct interpretations of Marxism-Leninism. The cases of Iran, Afghanistan, and Indonesia are illustrative.

In Iran there were many sources of opposition to the Shah's dictatorship. Arguably, the first anti-Shah demonstrations were organized by the salaried middle class and by intellectuals. Toward the end of the 1960s and in the early 1970s, underground political organizations arose with the aim of overthrowing the regime through a protracted armed struggle. They were inspired by "the victory of the armed struggle in Algeria and Cuba and also the experience of guerrilla warfare in Vietnam and Central America."[22]

The two most successful of these groups were the Fedaii Organization and the Mojahedin-e Khalq Organization. Both had great appeal among university students. The Fedaii Organization was strongly influenced by Regis Debray, the French advocate of armed struggle, who believed that the guerrilla organization was the nucleus of the revolutionary party and that through the course of the struggle, a party would be created to lead the revolution.[23]

The Mojahedin-e Khalq Organization also supported armed struggle in Iran. Followers believed that Islam and Marxism were compatible, regarding Islam as being in favor of the socialization of the means of production, elimination of exploitation, and the creation of a classless society. Together, the Fedaii and Mojahedin carried out many successful attacks on the security forces of the regime. They assassinated

---

[21] Ibid., p. 54.
[22] Mohammed Amjad, *Iran* (Westport, Conn.: Greenwood Press, 1989), p. 105.
[23] Ibid., pp. 105–106.

the chief military prosecutor of Tehran, a police general, several SAVAK (secret police) agents, and three American military advisers.[24]

The regime was able to suppress brutally these organizations. By 1976, more than 90 percent of the founders and original members of both organizations had been executed or were in prison.[25] This suppression constrained their ideas from gaining currency, but their attacks on the regime surely served as a catalyst for the politicization of Iran in the 1970s. Several factors explain the success of Islam as a revolutionary force where Marxism-Leninism had failed. The clerics in Iran had a wider and more effective organizational base than the Marxists from which to mobilize popular opposition to the Shah. And Islam had a resonance and legitimacy with the entire population that Marxism-Leninism could only aspire to have. Finally, the moral authority of Islam protected the clerics from the kind of brutal suppression encountered earlier by secular organizations.

Despite the eminence of the clerics, and of the Ayatollah Khomaini in particular, strife continued after the Shah's departure in February 1979. A plethora of political parties and movements, including the Fedaii and the Mojahedin, advocated a variety of radical policies. At times there was consensus between the clerics and the radicals, as on the desirability of harsh retribution for the accomplices of the Shah.[26] There were also attempts to build bridges between Marxism and Islam. For example, a journal highly influential among the young, *Ommat* (*The Community*), advocated socialist policies, Islam, and anti-imperialism. Nonetheless, conflict between contending political forces sometimes erupted into pitched street battles.

The clerics managed to consolidate their authority in part because of their superior strength, but also because of external threats to the country. In November 1979 about four hundred pro-Khomaini students took over the American embassy in Tehran and held American diplomats and military personnel hostage.

> The embassy takeover gave a boost to . . . Ayatollah Khomaini. The foreign enemy and the danger of an imminent U.S. attack were utilized to rally the masses behind the regime. This took the thunder away from the left. . . . The embassy takeover also caused confusion among the leftist forces. Some regarded it as a genuine anti-imperialist struggle that would result in the radicalization of the society. Some others simply supported this action to relieve themselves from the accusation of complicity with the United States.[27]

[24] Ibid., pp. 106–107.
[25] Ibid., p. 107.
[26] Shaul Bakhash, *The Reign of the Ayatollahs*, rev. ed. (New York: Basic Books, 1990), p. 62.
[27] Amjad, *Iran*, p. 140.

The invasion of Iran by Iraq in September 1980 further strengthened the clerics and undermined the radicals. Iranians were asked to join the revolutionary guards and the army to defend the "Islamic homeland."[28]

While the left lost its bid for control of the state, it nonetheless exerted substantial, and perhaps decisive, influence over Marxists' greatest passion—economics. Iran's economic policies came to resemble those of other contemporary revolutions. Shaul Bakhash summarizes the revamping of the Iranian economy:

> Some measures were adopted to ameliorate the lot of the poor and to spread economic opportunities. But these had only limited impact. More significantly, the government took over large sectors of the economy through nationalization and expropriation, including banking, insurance, major industry, large-scale agriculture and construction, and an important part of foreign trade. It also involved itself in the domestic distribution of goods. As a result, the economic role of the state was greatly swollen and that of the private sector greatly diminished by the revolution.[29]

Explaining the impact of Marxist ideas on economic decisions is difficult. Part of the explanation is that Islam has more to say about cultural issues (including gender relations) than it does about the organization of the economy. As in Ethiopia, those in opposition to radical students and intellectuals attempted to disarm them by appropriating their ideas.[30] Finally, the political activity of the left generated popular support for nationalization, land reform, and other measures associated with socialism. In sum, the Iranian revolution was an Islamic revolution, but in Iran there was, as elsewhere, an intellectual culture of Marxism. The adherents of this culture lost many savage battles, but they helped make the revolution possible and shaped postrevolutionary Iran.

In Afghanistan, the same coexistence of a centuries-old Islam and a newly appropriated Marxism-Leninism existed. But here the roles were reversed. The People's Democratic Party of Afghanistan (PDPA) was formed by a small group of Marxist intellectuals in early 1965.[31] In April 1978 the party seized control of the state through a military coup, and committed the country to a socialist revolution. The party's claimed membership at the time of the revolution was between 7,000

---

[28] Ibid., p. 144.

[29] Bakhash, *The Reign of the Ayatollahs*, p. 166.

[30] Hooshang Amirahmadi, *Revolution and Economic Transition* (Albany: State University of New York Press, 1990), p. 24.

[31] Girish Mathur, *New Afghanistan* (New Delhi: Sterling Publishers, 1983), p. 75.

and 10,000, and roughly half of these members resided in Kabul.[32] The party had not set up even one peasant's organization across the length and breadth of Afghanistan, even though peasants comprised 85 percent of the national population.[33] Resistance to the PDPA's reforms led to a counterrevolution in which Islam provided the intellectual opposition to the regime's Marxism. Soviet intervention to aid the beleaguered government provoked a fervent nationalist backlash.

Islam was also important in challenging Dutch colonialism in Indonesia. According to George Kahin:

> Danger to Dutch ascendancy in the Indies came not so much from the Pan-Islamic ideas that Indonesian students at Mecca brought back with them . . . as from the Modernist Islamic ideas taught in Cairo.[34]

> Modernist political and social ideas entered the country and exerted a tremendous influence, finally manifesting themselves in the first powerful Indonesian nationalist movement, the Sarekat Islam. It was the nationalistic, anti-imperialist, and socialistically inclined program of this movement, rather than the ideas of Pan-Islam, which was the "epidemic" that attacked so considerable a part of the Indonesian population.[35]

However, Kahin suggests that "Western education"—including that provided in the Netherlands—was more responsible for the spread of nationalistic and revolutionary doctrines than was Islamic schooling. Furthermore, Western education offered a political alternative to colonialism—socialism. For Indonesian students, "The appeal of Leninist Marxism was especially strong."[36] The Indonesian Communist Party (PKI) came to be the largest Communist party after its counterparts in the Soviet Union and China, and it was the most powerful political party in Indonesia.[37] The party's bitterly contested bid for power complicated Indonesia's politics for decades.

By comparison, the concurrent revolutions in the Americas show how, in the absence of an alternative intellectual force like Islam, Marxist radical initiatives are more readily successful. In Grenada, revolution was stimulated by a fashion for Marxism-Leninism among dissident intellectuals, in combination with an appreciation for the civil

---

[32] Raja Anwar, *The Tragedy of Afghanistan*, trans. Khalid Hasan (London: Verso, 1988), p. 138.

[33] Ibid., p. 110.

[34] George Kahin, *Nationalism and Revolution in Indonesia* (Ithaca: Cornell University Press, 1952), pp. 45–46.

[35] Ibid., p. 48.

[36] Ibid., p. 51.

[37] Ruth McVey, *The Rise of Indonesian Communism* (Ithaca: Cornell University Press, 1965), p. vii.

rights and black power movements in the United States. The general political culture of Grenada and the political preparation of the two most important leaders of the New Jewel Movement, which seized power in 1979, is summarized by Gordon Lewis:

> The Grenadian progressive movement was influenced, naturally enough, by the general liberalizing influence of the Black Power Movement of the time, as well as by the ideological influence of the Cuban Revolution. The Rodney "riots" of 1968 in Jamaica and the "February revolution" of 1970 in Trinidad were influenced by the Black Power and militant civil rights movements in the United States, which in turn influenced the Grenada radicals. Both Maurice Bishop and Bernard Coard belonged to the group of young people of the West Indian "brain drain," encountering all of these movements in their studies abroad. . . . Education, indeed, was a vital factor.[38]

The rapid growth of both higher and secondary education in the post–World War II period helped generate in Grenada a more informed group of younger people, who were more susceptible to radical ideas.

In Nicaragua, there was also a revolution in 1979. And here, too, the role of students and intellectuals was decisive. The Sandinista National Liberation Front (FSLN) was founded in 1961 by three former student activists. Two of the three were introduced to Marxism in the early 1950s by a mutual friend who had been to Guatemala, where the reformist regime of Jacobo Arbenz had made Marxist writings available. And a local writer allowed the youths to use his personal library, which included such books as Nikolai Bukharin's 1919 textbook on the Bolshevik program, *The ABC of Communism*.[39]

Throughout its history, the majority of the FSLN's members entered the organization through the student movement. One veteran, Doris María Tijerino, explained how students had come to occupy such a prominent role in the organization:

> The students, because of their privileged position in the country, because of their access to culture and knowledge of the revolutionary experience of other countries, have often been the first to commit themselves to revolutionary theories. Study at the university pushes them toward revolutionary consciousness.[40]

[38] Gordon Lewis, *Grenada* (Baltimore: Johns Hopkins University Press, 1987), pp. 17–18.

[39] David Nolan, *The Ideology of the Sandinistas and the Nicaraguan Revolution* (Graduate School of International Studies, University of Miami, Coral Gables, 1984), p. 19.

[40] Margaret Randall, *Somos millones* (Mexico City: Editorial Extemporáneos, 1977), pp. 123–124.

Pictures of ranking Sandinistas on display at the Museum of the Revolution in Managua are illuminating. Taken in the 1960s, the pictures reveal students with long hair, sideburns, moustaches, and beards. All the hair, and the style in which it is brandished, attest to the awareness among Nicaraguan youth in the 1960s and 1970s of what their peers were up to in places as distant as Berkeley and Paris.

In 1986, a New York journalist, Paul Berman, interviewed Omar Cabezas, a Sandinista leader and the author of a celebrated memoir of guerrilla life.[41] Their discussion and Berman's conclusions are generalizable:

> Cabezas was happy to reminisce. . . . He brought up names like Danny Cohn-Bendit, the Paris student leader of 1968. Berkeley and Kent State came to his lips. When the Kent students were massacred in 1970, Cabezas organized a memorial meeting at León. . . . I think he wanted it understood that he and his comrades weren't as isolated as might be imagined. They were part of the big world. They knew what was happening in the main centers of the New Left. But if this was his thought, it was, of course, a strange delusion. For Paris and Berkeley were obviously not, in retrospect, the world centers of the New Left. The uprisings at Columbia and the Sorbonne were not the crucial university rebellions.[42]

Fantasy in prosperous Western Europe and North America became realism in many poor countries of the world.

[41] Paul Berman, "Nicaragua 1986," *Mother Jones* (December 1986): 20–27, 53–54.
[42] Ibid., p. 20.

3

Seizing Power

THE PREVALENCE of an intellectual culture intoxicated with revolution, Marxism-Leninism, and socialism does not in itself explain either the sizable number of revolutions among the poorer countries in the aftermath of World War II or, more importantly, the configuration of countries that did and did not experience revolutions. Indeed, many states with a radical academic and intellectual community were unperturbed. The factors that generate revolutions are diverse. They include the shadowy world of ideas and human agency, but also regime legitimacy and performance, economic processes, and international strife. Conversely, no single problem or impetus is enough to undermine a status quo and replace it dramatically and irrevocably. Only when a number of processes interact is sufficient force unleashed to shatter and replace existing institutions. And the number and kind of forces necessary for a revolutionary conjuncture vary with the particularities of state, society, and economy.

Although the phenomenon of revolutions has attracted considerable study, no model with predictive capability has emerged. Alas, a "theory of revolutions" limited to actual occurrences is not a theory, but only a description. Still, it is illuminating to compare long-standing attempts to explain when and where revolutions occur (most of which are based on European cases) with the facts of revolution in the world's poor countries. Such a comparison helps highlight the variable sources of regime collapse and suggest ways in which contemporary revolutions may differ from such historical antecedents as the French and Russian revolutions.

Briefly put, the conclusion that emerges is that multiple kinds of regime crises have contributed to revolutions in poor countries. Those that seem most salient are crises of regime legitimacy. The regimes that have been judged most illegitimate, and have thus been most easily toppled by aggressive revolutionaries, are intransigent colonial governments and easily personified dictatorships. Victims of intransigent colonialism included Vietnam, Algeria, Angola, Guinea-Bissau, and Mozambique. It is noteworthy that the dissolution of the sprawling British Empire produced only a single, isolated revolution—in South Yemen. Elsewhere, British responsiveness to local demands, tardy as it sometimes was, diffused revolutionary aspirations and dampened those that might have arisen. Vilified dictators who were toppled include Fulgencio Batista in Cuba, Emperor Haile Selassie in Ethiopia, Anastasio Somoza in Nicaragua, and the Shah, Mohammad Reza Pahlavi, in Iran. A third characteristic contributing decisively to contemporary revolutions was the sheer absence of entrenched political institutions. In such countries as Benin and Madagascar, a military coup d'état alone proved sufficient to hurl their respective societies into radical transformations.

In the all-important case of China, the origins of revolution were quite complex, entangled in foreign occupation, war, and civil strife. Still, the structural origin of most contemporary revolutions was either opposition to entrenched colonialism or to a dictator, or a singular seizure of power by a handful of military officers and their compliant troops. Comparing the relatively large universe of contemporary revolutions with prevailing schools of thought about the causes of revolution does not challenge this interpretation. Moreover, the exercise reinforces the conclusion that while many poor countries may have inevitably been shaken by political crises in the decades after World War II, there was nothing foreordained about how these crises of government and economic development would be resolved. The aloofness and ideological dispositions of a narrow, urban, and literate elite aggravated many political crises and, more importantly, determined the course of political and economic change. One of the important ways ideology shaped choices was by inflating the perceived spectrum of possibilities.

Theories and Cases

Systematic attempts by American scholars to explain the origins and nature of revolutions have gone through three distinct phases, or "generations."[1] The first, extending from 1900 to 1940, included the work of Sorokin, Edwards, Pettee, and Brinton.[2] These scholars imaginatively explored the pattern of events found in historical revolutions. Although they had much to say about the origins of revolution, they emphasized the sequence of events in revolutions. Their work is rich with hypotheses, but there was little attempt to be theoretical. Crane

[1] Jack Goldstone, "Theories of Revolutions," *World Politics* 32 (April 1980): 425.

[2] Pitrim Sorokin, *The Sociology of Revolution* (Philadelphia: J. B. Lippincott, 1925); Lyford Edwards, *The Natural History of Revolution* (Chicago: University of Chicago Press, 1927); George Pettee, *The Process of Revolution* (New York: Harper, 1938); Crane Brinton, *The Anatomy of Revolution* (New York: W. W. Norton, 1938).

Brinton's insightful study, although published originally in 1938, is still read.[3]

The second generation, falling roughly between 1940 and 1975, included the work of Davies, Gurr, Johnson, Smelser, Huntington, and Tilly.[4] These scholars drew heavily on broad theories from psychology (cognitive psychology and frustration-aggression theory), sociology (structuralist-functionalist theory), and political science (the pluralist theory of interest-group competition and theories about modernization).[5]

> The second-generation theorists . . . saw the development of revolutionary situations as basically a two-step process. First a pattern of events arises that somehow marks a break or change from previous patterns. This change then affects some critical variable—the cognitive state of the masses, the equilibrium of the system, or the magnitude of conflict and resource control of competing interest groups. If the effect on the critical variable is of sufficient magnitude, a potentially revolutionary situation occurs.[6]

These scholars attempted to devise parsimonious social theory, but the explanatory power of their analyses is weak. In all of the theories, the critical variable is extremely difficult to measure. What society, for example, does not have widespread relative deprivation of one kind or another? And how can it be deduced whether or not a given social system is "synchronized"? Since it is not possible to measure either the cognitive state of mind of large masses of individuals, or the strain or disequilibrium of a social system, or the magnitude of goal conflict and resources of competing groups, it is difficult to ascertain a correlation between broadly defined constructs of "social change" and specific changes in critical variables.[7] Despite aspirations of scientific explanation, the theories are not falsifiable.

The third generation of scholarship grew out of the rising interest in Marxist theory and forms of analysis in the 1960s. This genre of scholarship includes the work of Moore, Wolf, Paige, Trimberger, and

---

[3] Intellectually, Brinton appears heavily indebted to the work of Edwards.

[4] James Davies, "Toward a Theory of Revolution," *American Sociological Review* 27 (February 1962): 5–19; Ted Gurr, *Why Men Rebel* (Princeton: Princeton University Press, 1970); Chalmers Johnson, *Revolutionary Change* (Boston: Little, Brown, 1966); Neil Smelser, *Theory of Collective Behavior* (New York: Free Press, 1963); Samuel Huntington, *Political Order in Changing Societies* (New Haven: Yale University Press, 1968); Charles Tilly, "Revolutions and Collective Violence," in Fred Greenstein and Nelson Polsby, eds., *Handbook of Political Science*, vol 3 (Reading, Mass.: Addison-Wesley, 1975), pp. 483–555.

[5] Jack Goldstone, "Theories of Revolution," p. 425.

[6] Ibid., pp. 429–430.

[7] Ibid., p. 431.

Skocpol.[8] Its initial focus was on class conflict, but as Marxist studies evolved, greater attention came to be paid to the variable goals and structures of states, and to the intrusion of international political and economic pressures on the domestic organization of societies.

This third generation of scholarship on revolution is similar to the first generation in that it is more historically grounded. As Skocpol wrote in her influential 1979 study, "Marxist theory works with less general, more historically grounded categories than the recent social-scientific theories."[9] Where Skocpol and her methodological kin differ from Brinton and his contemporaries are the formers' focus on the causes of revolutions and a faith, among the latter, as Skocpol says, that "social revolutions as such *can* be treated as theoretical subjects."[10] Believing it is possible to construct theories of revolutions puts Skocpol in the company of the second generation of scholarship on revolution. An even more important similarity is a shared emphasis, in discourse and explanation, on impersonal social structures. Only those writing at the beginning of the century put much stock in the power of revolutionaries and their ideas.

The abundance and diversity of studies of revolutions provide a mixed blessing. It makes it difficult to choose among the myriad of competing and sometimes contradictory hypotheses about the causes of revolution. In a review of the literature on the causes of revolution, Harry Eckstein noted, "Scarcely anything in the French *ancien régime* has not been blamed, by one writer or another, for the revolution, and all of their interpretations, however contradictory, are based on solid facts."[11] Eckstein goes on to chronicle fifteen general hypotheses about the cause of the French Revolution. And while that revolution is the most studied case, "even . . . the Chinese Communist Revolution has given rise to a fearful number of plausible hypotheses, many directly contradictory."[12]

Eckstein does not offer a solution to this embarrassment of interpretative riches. But he imposes some order on the chaos of hypotheses by categorizing them into preconditions or precipitants, insurgents or incumbents, and structural or behavioral hypotheses.[13] Finally, he raises

[8] Barrington Moore, Jr., *Social Origins of Dictatorship and Democracy* (Boston: Beacon Press, 1966); Eric Wolf, *Peasant Wars of the Twentieth Century* (New York: Harper & Row, 1969); Jeffrey Paige, *Agrarian Revolution* (New York: Free Press, 1975); Kay Trimberger, *Revolution from Above* (New Brunswick, N.J.: Transaction Books, 1978); Theda Skocpol, *States and Social Revolutions* (Cambridge: Cambridge University Press, 1979).

[9] Theda Skocpol, *States and Social Revolutions*, p. 34.

[10] Ibid., p. 35.

[11] Harry Eckstein, "On the Etiology of Internal Wars," *History and Theory* 4 (1965): 137.

[12] Ibid., p. 138.

[13] Ibid., pp. 139–159.

the often overlooked question of the obstacles to revolution. Surely, revolutions occur not only because forces leading toward them are strong, but also because forces tending to inhibit, or obstruct, them are weak or absent. Answering the question of why revolutions have occurred invariably leads to the question of why they did not occur elsewhere.

A "precipitant" is an event that actually starts a revolution; "preconditions" are those circumstances that make it possible for the precipitants to bring about political violence. Eckstein suggests:

> The distinction between precipitants and preconditions can ... prevent much pointless argument between those who stress short-run setbacks and those who emphasize long-term trends in the etiology of civil strife. Clearly no internal war can occur without precipitant events to set it off; and clearly no precipitants can set off internal war unless the conditions of society make it possible for them to do so. The greatest service that the distinction between precipitants and preconditions of internal war can render, however, is to shift attention from aspects of internal war which defy analysis to those which are amenable to systematic inquiry. Phenomena which precipitate internal war are almost always unique and ephemeral in character.[14]

The distinction between precipitants and preconditions helps to organize an inquiry into certain contemporary revolutions and, importantly, suggests the novelty of some of them.

The precipitants of many contemporary revolutions are easily identified and readily agreed upon. They include, for example, in Guinea-Bissau, the 1959 massacre of Pidgiguiti, during which Portuguese colonialists killed and wounded dozens of striking dock and transport workers. In Ethiopia, the drought of 1972–1973 was a precipitant of revolution. The assassination of the popular newspaper editor, Pedro Joaquín Chamorro, in the streets of Managua, was a precipitant of the Nicaraguan Revolution. Yet in these three cases, and in still others, one must consider also broader causes—or preconditions—of revolution.

In a number of contemporary revolutions, the apparent precipitant of revolution—a military coup d'état—upon closer inspection proves to be a cause. Given the underdevelopment and fragility of governmental institutions in poor countries, a military coup was sometimes enough, if its leaders were so inclined, to launch a radical revamping of society and state. Benin, for example, became independent (under the name Dahomey) from France in 1960, and in the ensuing twelve years it experienced five "palace coups." But a sixth coup in October 1972 by (then) Major Mathieu Kérékou led to the recasting of state and society:

---

[14] Ibid., p. 140.

Kérékou declared that Dahomey was to become a "Marxist-Leninist state" and two days later announced that the nation's banks, insurance companies, and oil-distribution facilities would be nationalized. Subsequently, he ordered the establishment of "Defense of the Revolution Committees" in all businesses to "protect the revolution from sabotage." . . . [T]he country was styled a "people's republic" to reflect the ideology officially embraced a year earlier, and was renamed Benin. . . . The Benin People's Revolutionary Party (PRPB) was established as the nucleus of a one-party system.[15]

It is impossible to find harbingers—or preconditions—of what would emerge from the October 1972 coup in Benin.

The revolution in Benin was made possible by the weakness of political institutions, a weakness that enabled a determined cabal in command of the official instruments of coercion to throw society into upheaval. Yet this fragility of government had long existed; it was not noticeably different at the time of revolution from the time of the earlier coups. Benin's West African neighbors had also experienced poverty and political instability, leading to repeated coups d'état, but without succumbing to revolution.

The case of Madagascar is similar to that of Benin. Revolution arrived via a failed coup in early 1975 that unleashed a rapid chain of events. The country had four heads of state in four months, the last of whom launched Madagascar on a course of socialist transformation.

In other cases, coups d'état have a political origin. These cases include those of Egypt in 1952, Burma in 1962, Ethiopia in 1974, Afghanistan in 1978, and Grenada in 1979. In these latter cases, the coups d'etat seem to be more precipitants than the sole, almost freakish, causes of revolution as in Benin and Madagascar.

The preconditions for revolution in Egypt, for example, were numerous. King Farouk is described in terms recalling Louis XVI: "He had a flawed character, surrounding himself with corrupt advisers and flatterers, and his private life became a scandal."[16] The upper strata of society were conspicuous in their consumption and invisible in their contribution to society. Intellectuals were alienated from the regime. There was a terrible cholera epidemic. The continued presence of the British, made visible by their troops, was a national affront. The mauling of the Egyptian army in the 1948 war over Palestine was blamed on the king and his government.[17]

After gaining independence from the British in 1948, Burma maintained a parliamentary democracy for a decade. The 1962 coup that led

[15] Arthur Banks, ed., *Political Handbook of the World* (Binghamton, N.Y.: CSA Publications, 1991), p. 67.

[16] Derek Hopwood, *Egypt*, 3d ed. (London: HarperCollins, 1991), p. 21.

[17] Ibid., pp. 2–32.

to a revamping of Burma was certainly inspired at least in part by decreasing government effectiveness in solving problems of internal security, national unity, and economic development. In Afghanistan, political restiveness was aggravated by recurrent famine and public impatience with successive governments' inability to promote sustained economic development. Many Grenadians were strongly opposed to their prime minister, Eric Gairy, whom they compared to Haiti's infamous dictator, "Papa Doc" Duvalier.

Despite these and still other "preconditions" of revolution in the five countries, it is significant that (1) the decisions to launch revolutions were made by small groups of individuals who had considerable political autonomy; (2) these same preconditions were evident in many—if not most—other poor countries during the same time period; and (3) ruling governments confronted with these potential preconditions of revolution did not have adequate resources to thwart revolutionary assault.

Contemporary revolutions originating in struggles against colonial domination appear more complex than those resulting from a military coup. Especially in cases of intransigent colonialism, these newer revolutions seem less voluntaristic. Put another way, responsibility for the revolution seems traceable to both the "incumbents" and the "insurgents." Racism and economic exploitation have engendered resentment and anger. Still, European efforts to mask the deleterious effects of colonialism and to suppress dissent were long effective in many locales, necessitating political agitation on the part of aspiring revolutionaries.

The relationship between colonialism and liberation struggles is illuminated in Mozambique by a FRELIMO militant, Gabriel Maurício Nantimbo:

> Previously I was in a state of servitude, but I didn't know it. I thought that was just how the world was. I didn't know that Mozambique was our country. The books said we were Portuguese. Then about 1961 I began to hear other things. The old men in their cooperatives were also beginning to agitate. In 1962 even the children saw the truth.[18]

This account from Mozambique suggests it was not always self-evident that an alternative to colonialism existed, or how an alternative could be pursued. Also, there were often fears of colonial reprisals and uncertainty about just what an alternative to colonialism entailed. Finally, in many countries, large segments of the population found colonialism "agreeable." In Algeria, for example:

[18] Eduardo Mondlane, *The Struggle for Mozambique* (Harmondsworth, Middlesex, England: Penguin, 1969), p. 127.

The brilliance and spiritual vigor of France were magnetic, attracting the Algerians in spite of themselves. . . . How else can we explain why, during the seven-and-a-half years of war, the overwhelming majority of Algerians cooperated with the French? Some, it is true, did so passively rather than actively, some out of fear or ignorance; but, nevertheless, the French were able to enroll no less than 200,000 Algerians as officials . . . to help them in the struggle against the revolutionary minority.[19]

Before revolutionaries could launch a successful armed struggle against even the most obdurate colonialists, they had to engage in tireless political education.

For Amílcar Cabral in Guinea-Bissau, resistance to colonialism began with the struggle to win back "historical dignity," to promote "re-Africanization":

[T]he history of [colonial] liberation struggles shows that they have generally been preceded by an upsurge of cultural manifestations, which progressively harden into an attempt, successful or not, to assert the cultural personality of the dominated people by an act of denial of the culture of the oppressor.[20]

In the bid to build a revolutionary movement, Cabral and his colleagues sought to win allegiance among the rural poor, in part by banning forced marriages, providing rudimentary social services, and promising a better material life if the African Party for the Independence of Guinea and Cape Verde (PAIGC) was successful in ousting the Portuguese. Cabral admitted, "The people are not fighting for ideas, for the things in anyone's head. They are fighting to win material benefits, to live better and in peace, to see their lives go forward."[21] Thus, the effort to end intransigent colonialism, such as that of the Portuguese in southern Africa, involved both discrediting the institutions of colonialism and providing an alternative, and more appealing, conception of state and society.

The evils of colonialism provided fertile ground for aspiring revolutionaries. Efforts by colonialists to repress growing dissent usually only inflamed and radicalized liberation movements. And because of transparent ethnic and class divisions, colonialists were always a conspicuous target. Yet, a comparative review of revolutionary struggles against colonialism—in lusophone Africa, in Algeria, and Vietnam—highlights how colonialism did not fall from its own weight. Insurgents were indispensable, not just to tackle the might of colonial armies but to enlist widespread public support for their cause as well.

[19] Arslan Humbaraci, *Algeria* (New York: Praeger, 1966), p. 25.

[20] Carlos Lopes, *Guinea-Bissau* (Boulder, Colo.: Westview Press, 1987), p. 52.

[21] Basil Davidson, *The Liberation of Guiné*, p. 58.

The struggle for liberation was always as much a political as a military challenge.

Since uprisings against colonialism were not spontaneous, but had to be instigated, political organization and leadership were necessary. The social base of that leadership was consistently narrow. Amílcar Cabral poignantly suggested the dilemma of liberation struggles against colonialism. In Guinea-Bissau, and elsewhere, colonialism stifled the development of a national "bourgeoisie" and "proletariat":

> Under these conditions, the character of the revolution becomes a distinctive one in so far as the forces of the revolution are predominantly rural, and the leadership of the revolution is located not in those classes traditionally identified by Marxist theory but in a social stratum whose special position within colonialism inevitably drives it to raise the banner of national liberation.[22]

For Cabral, the urban "petit bourgeoisie" became revolutionary as a result of the racial humiliation and social degradation it suffers at the hands of the colonial authorities. Cabral never provided much definition of just who constituted the "petit bourgeoisie," but in the case of Guinea-Bissau revolutionary leadership was drawn overwhelmingly from the sons and daughters of teachers, small-shop owners, nurses, and the others who were able to provide an education for their children. Differences in social class and education led not only to differing tolerance for the evils of colonialism but also to differing views of how state and society should be remade in the aftermath of colonialism. (Herein were sown seeds of future conflict.)

The third common origin of contemporary revolutions is the ouster of despots. Many parallels can be drawn between these insurrections and the anticolonialist liberation struggles. First, while easily personified and easily caricatured dictators served as visible targets for public frustration and hostility, their presence alone was not enough to engender revolutions. Second, while there were many instances of spontaneous public acts of rebellion, all of the insurrections were instigated and encouraged, if not led, by a narrow segment of society, typically young, urban, and comparatively well educated. Finally, insurrections were successful when broad social coalitions could be formed that cut across occupational and class divisions.

The Cuban and Nicaraguan cases are illustrative. In both countries, organized opposition began with students. In Cuba, the University of Havana was long "a center of ideological preaching and political in-

---

[22] Dessalegn Rahmato, *Cabral and the Problem of the African Revolution* (Addis Ababa: Institute of Development Research, 1982), p. 14

volvement."[23] Fidel Castro's famous guerrilla columns in the Sierra Maestra were composed largely of former university students and were led exclusively by them. The rebels were not *from* the mountains; they went *to* the mountains. And their peers in Havana staged almost daily demonstrations, many of which ended in violent clashes with the police. Bombs exploded in Havana, and political assassinations were commonplace. Rural and, especially, urban violence exposed the illegitimacy and incompetence of the Batista regime. Popular discontent with the dictatorship grew toward open rebellion. Castro's troops, nicknamed the "bearded ones," reportedly never numbered more than three thousand, suggesting that the Batista regime had not so much toppled as collapsed. Yet Castro and his urban and rural brethren were the sparks needed to ignite popular and international discontent.

The Nicaraguan Revolution, which ousted the Somoza dictatorship in July of 1979, was a broad-based insurrection that enjoyed widespread popular support. The armed vanguard of the struggle, the Sandinista National Liberation Front (FSLN), had been formed in 1961 and had tenaciously survived numerous setbacks. While the FSLN had worked for years building popular support in rural areas, the decisive battles of the insurrection were fought in cities. The critical support for the FSLN's final campaign came not from peasants but from urban youth. Indeed, the average age of combatants was said to have been only sixteen, explaining why the Sandinistas and their followers were nicknamed *los muchachos* (the boys).[24]

The inequities and injustices of the Somoza regime made many, if not most, Nicaraguan peasants and rural laborers sympathetic to the FSLN's cause. However, while a few joined the FSLN's ranks, most of the rural poor remained reluctant to participate in politics. In this caution about radical political change, they were similar to their counterparts in other poor rural societies. Supposedly, Ernesto "Che" Guevara's guerrilla diary, captured by the Bolivian army, contains bitter complaints about the indifference of the local peasants to revolution: "The inhabitants of this region are as impenetrable as rocks. You speak to them, but in the deepness of their eyes you note they do not believe you."[25] An old Central American peasant adage explains the attitude of many poor rural dwellers: "Better a familiar evil than an unfamiliar blessing."

---

[23] Mario Llerena, *The Unsuspected Revolution* (Ithaca: Cornell University Press, 1978), p. 39.

[24] See Humberto Ortega, *50 años de lucha sandinista* (Mexico City: Editorial Diogenes, 1979); and Fernando Carmona, ed., *Nicaragua* (Mexico City: Editorial Nuestro Tiempo, 1980).

[25] Norman Gall, "The Legacy of Che Guevara," *Commentary* 44 (December 1967): 31.

Although the peasantry in most cases have been reluctant participants in revolutionary movements, in countries where central government and landlord authority have decayed, peasants often cooperate
passively with guerrillas, allowing them freedom of movement.[26] In
such cases, authorities searching for aspiring revolutionaries are
greeted with feigned ignorance.[27] This kind of tacit peasant support
was granted to the guerrilla movements in lusophone Africa and to
guerrillas in Cuba and Nicaragua.

The most acclaimed account of the Nicaraguan Revolution, both
within Nicaragua and abroad, is the autobiography of a combatant,
Omar Cabezas. The literal translation of the title of his book is "The
mountain is something more than an immense green steppe."[28]
Cabezas recounts being a student activist in the university city of León,
of being drafted into the FSLN, of the mystique of going up into the
unknown mountains, and of there meeting a legendary *comandante*
(another former university student), who was perched on a rock reading a dense Marxist tract.

Cabezas's memoirs make it poignantly clear that he and most
everyone else (in contrast to the studious *comandante*) fought not *for*
something but only *against* something—against the Somoza family
and their repressive National Guard. The same pattern was reported
in Cuba: "[S]trong-man rule was abhorrent to the vast majority of the
Cuban people. . . . All during the rest of the 1950s the popular revolutionary appeal . . . focused on the elimination of Batista and his dictatorship. That was 'revolution' for most people."[29] Similarly, in the colonial liberation struggle the aim of the overwhelming majority of
those who committed themselves to the struggle was simply to oust
the colonialists. Specific plans for what would follow either the ousting
of colonialists or the toppling of despots were the domain of the revolutionary leadership—invariably a small handful of individuals.

The key to successful insurrections has not been, as is so often ro-
manticized, an alliance between guerrillas and peasants. Instead, what
has been indispensable is the ability of revolutionaries to weld together a broad coalition of groups—large segments of the middle class,
the peasantry, and foreign interests.[30] The building of a broad, cross-

[26] Timothy Wickham-Crowley, *Exploring Revolution* (Armonk, N.Y.: M. E. Sharpe,
1991), p. 51.

[27] The political repertoire of peasants is discussed in James Scott, *Weapons of the Weak*
(New Haven: Yale University Press, 1985).

[28] Omar Cabezas, *La montaña es algo más que una inmensa estepa verde* (Havana: Casa de
las Américas, 1982).

[29] Mario Llerena, *The Unsuspected Revolution*, p. 42.

[30] Robert Dix, "Why Revolutions Succeed and Fail," *Polity* 16 (Spring 1984): 432–435.

class coalition of opposition would not have been possible if revolutionary elites had revealed their ultimate aspirations to revamp ambitiously state and society.

Symbiotic Political Dynamics

Revolutionary politics is crucial to explaining the origin of contemporary revolutions. The importance of agency is attested to by (1) the number of contemporary revolutions that began without recognizable preconditions—those that were simply the outcome of a military coup; and (2) the sustained role played by revolutionary leadership and organization in other cases, in which preconditions (colonialism or a dictatorship) existed. The decisive role played by agency underlies Eckstein's claim that hypotheses about the origin and course of contemporary revolutions need to be "behavioral" (as opposed to "structural").

Yet agency alone cannot explain the configuration of revolutions. "Structures," particularly the institutions of government, are important too. From 1945 to 1990 at least, revolutions only occurred where there was a congruence of behavioral forces and structural preconditions. Just as there can be no revolution without revolutionaries, so revolutions of an insurrectionary nature (as opposed to those that begin as a military coup) have not been possible in the absence of either colonialism or a vilified dictator. Without these structural conditions, the appeals of aspiring revolutionaries fall on deaf ears.

It is worth emphasizing that the determinant structural characteristics are all political, revolving around the kind of government in power and its style of governing. There are no readily apparent socioeconomic characteristics that distinguish the countries in which revolutionary movements have succeeded from those in which they have failed. No persuasive propositions emerge from an examination of comparative levels of economic and social development—as measured by such indicators as gross national product per capita, percentage of the labor force employed in agriculture, the degree of urbanization, or the adult literacy rate.[31] There are no "automatic triggers."[32]

The case of Argentina illustrates the futility of revolutionary struggle in the absence of an easily identified and widely disdained target of wrath. While guerrilla groups were not unknown in Argentina before 1970, the earlier groups exerted little impact on national politics.

---

[31] Ibid., pp. 426–427.
[32] Lawrence Stone, "Theories of Revolution," *World Politics* 18 (October 1965): 166.

But by the end of 1970, there were three guerrilla groups, the most famous of which came to be the Montoneros. The guerrillas staged kidnappings, bank robberies, assassinations of senior army and police personnel, and escapades in which multinational corporations were forced to make charity donations to shantytowns in return for abducted executives. These guerrilla bands were composed overwhelmingly of lapsed students and newly qualified members of the professions, many from affluent middle-class families and nearly all in their early twenties.[33] Their inspiration is suggested by V. S. Naipaul:

> What had driven them to their cause? There would have been the element of mimicry, the wish not to be left out of the political current of the 1960s. "What the students say in America, they want to make concrete here"—I was told this in 1972 by a woman whose guerrilla nephew had been killed by the police: the young man had taken his revolution more seriously than the American students whose equal he wanted to be.[34]

The Montoneros and other guerrilla groups were committed to destroying "oligarchy," to expelling "foreign monopolies," and to provoking a crisis in capitalism that would usher in a socialist revolution. They failed. They were defeated in part by savage police and army repression, but also because Argentinians could not be roused against something so diffuse as the oligarchy, or for something so vague and uncertain as socialism.

In the aftermath of the Second World War, revolution came into vogue in university and intellectual circles in Western Europe and North America and concurrently throughout most of Latin America, Africa, the Middle East, and Asia. It gathered momentum, reaching its intellectual zenith in the late 1960s and early 1970s. As a former Argentine guerrilla, discussing his past, told Naipaul: "Peripheric countries like ours receive very clearly what is thought in the northern hemisphere. 'Liberation' was the word."[35]

Dreams of revolutions spread not only because of fashion but because of the horrors of colonialism, dictatorship, economic exploitation, and poverty. In a surprising number of the poorer countries of the world, a combination of inspirational leadership and the structural preconditions of a political powder keg enabled young intellectuals with ambitious ideas, abstracted from the writings of nineteenth- and early-twentieth-century European philosophers, to seize power.

---

[33] David Rock, *Argentina* (Berkeley: University of California Press, 1985), pp. 353–354.
[34] V. S. Naipaul, "Argentina," *New York Review of Books* 39 (30 January 1992): 13.
[35] Ibid., p. 14.

4

State-Building

IN HIS COMPARISON of European revolutions, Crane Brinton identified a pronounced and intriguing uniformity: a shift in power from moderates to extremists in the aftermath of victory.

> The honeymoon was in these revolutions short; very soon after the old regime had fallen there began to be evident signs that the victors were not so unanimous about what was to be done to remake the country as had appeared in the first triumphant speeches and ceremonies. Those who had directly taken over the mechanism of government were ... men of the kind usually called moderates. They represented the richer, better known, and higher placed of the old opposition to the government.... They found against them an increasingly strong and intransigent group of radicals and extremists who insisted that the moderates were trying to stop the revolution.... [T]here came a show of force ... and the moderates were beaten.... The extremists in their turn took power.[1]

Brinton convincingly argues that as power moves to the radicals, it gets more and more concentrated, and has a narrower social base. Power becomes more concentrated, in large part, because at each important crisis the defeated group is forced to drop out of politics.[2]

Moderates' adherence to compromise, common sense, toleration, and comfort makes them ineffectual in solving the trenchant problems that confront postrevolutionary polities. Moderates are also jostled by extremists, who inevitably are "better organized, more aggressive, and perhaps more unscrupulous."[3] Brinton is impressed by extremists' small numbers, but wryly concludes this is a source of strength.

> Great numbers are almost as unwieldy in politics as on the battlefield. In the politics of revolutions what counts is the ability to move swiftly, to make clear and final decisions, to push ... without regard for injured human dispositions. For such a purpose the active political group must be small. You cannot otherwise obtain the single-mindedness and devotion, the energy

[1] Crane Brinton, *The Anatomy of Revolution* (New York: W. W. Norton, 1938), pp. 149–150.
[2] Ibid., p. 150.
[3] Ibid., p. 158.

and the discipline, necessary to defeat the moderates. . . . The masses do not make revolutions. They may be enlisted for some impressive pageantry once the active few have won the revolution. But the impressive demonstrations the camera records . . . ought not to deceive the careful student of politics. . . . [Victory is] achieved by small, disciplined, principled, fanatical bodies.[4]

Revolutionary politics may resemble a courtroom in its dramatic intimacy.

"The accession of the extremists" is the most evident parallel between such European revolutions as the French and Russian and the many contemporary revolutions in the poor countries of the world. As argued in the previous chapter, revolutions have proven possible when a broad coalition of diverse strata and groups unite to topple an erstwhile regime deemed illegitimate. In recent cases of revolution, though, there is the same pattern of the triumphant coalitions fracturing, and of moderate governments representing the diversity of the coalition being replaced by a narrow government in pursuit of its own self-defined agenda.

The reasons for the failure of contemporary "moderate" revolutionaries and their ensuing replacement by "extremists" are similar to those of their historical precedents. However, the vogue of socialist ideology instills a clearer distinction between "moderates" and extremists. It inflames extremists and provides them with a plan—no matter how vague or incomplete—of the institutional design of a truly revolutionary state and of the multifaceted roles that the state should play in radically remaking society. Thus, the central division that usually emerges after the colonialists or the despot is ousted is between those who are for such vague prescripts as "peace and prosperity" and those who are for socialism. And when socialism dominates the normative landscape, the split is between those who imagine socialism à la the social democratic parties of Scandinavia and those with visions of the Bolsheviks, Lenin, and even Stalin.

The important exception is Iran, where the moderates were confronted by two groups of extremists: one bound to socialism, and another, more powerful set attached to Islam. Another variation occurred in the Bolivian and Egyptian revolutions of 1952, where no single ideology dominated. Although in 1962 Nasser and his colleagues proclaimed that Egypt was to embark on a course based on the principles of "scientific socialism," initially they seem to have been guided only by a diffuse desire for radical change. This desire was certainly inspired in part by socialism, but it was at heart nationalist and

[4] Ibid., p. 186.

populist.[5] Similarly, the National Revolutionary Movement (MNR) in Bolivia had at best an inchoate ideology. Even these cases, though, shared the hallmarks of what socialism came to stand for in the poorer parts of the world: anti-imperialism, anticapitalism, faith in state-led development, and an embrace of authoritarian rule supported by a single, mass-based political party.

The vanguard role usually played by committed socialists in inciting armed revolt not only made them the catalysts and linchpins of revolutionary coalitions, but it also left them well positioned to consolidate power in the aftermath of victory. Leaders of armed guerrilla organizations almost invariably have ended up heading the states that emerged subsequent to their victory. Because it is the guerrillas who ultimately defeat the government's forces and seize its institutions, the most viable resources through which political power can be exercised are at their disposal. The guerrillas have a likely monopoly on the instruments of coercion—the guns—and are adept at using and manipulating organizations.[6]

In the aftermath of victory, though, the task of armed guerrilla organizations shifts from marrying disparate political tendencies (including that of apathy) to consolidating their own power. Considerable political skill is necessary. The range of ways in which power may become consolidated by radicals in contemporary revolutions is suggested by the three cases of China, Ethiopia, and Nicaragua.

Mao Zedong did not hide his commitment to socialism during the prolonged war against the Nationalist government. But it is instructive that he felt compelled to win support—or at least neutralize potential opposition—by promising private enterprise a positive role in the new China.[7] Such a gesture was important, since the Chinese Communist Party had been out of touch with the cities since 1930. Still, when Mao's army occupied the cities in 1949, fear and chaos reigned. Government and urban services had broken down. Food shortages and inflation had created great hardship. The Communists immediately began to reestablish public order by introducing military government. Although an effort was made to break with the structure of the Nationalist government, continuity was maintained in the police.[8]

The historical environment in which the Chinese Communist Party had developed made the party dependent on the support, or at least the acquiescence, of the peasantry. Here, goodwill had been cultivated

[5] Derek Hopwood, *Egypt*, 3d ed. (London: HarperCollins, 1991), p. 90.

[6] Mehran Kamrava, *Revolutionary Politics* (Westport, Conn.: Praeger, 1992), p. 66.

[7] Franz Schurmann, *Ideology and Organization in Communist China*, rev. ed. (Berkeley: University of California Press, 1966), p. 221.

[8] Ibid., p. 371.

by improvised agrarian reform that curtailed the power and land-ownership of the gentry. Only when political power was consolidated, in large part through control of the cities, did Mao initiate the collectivization of Chinese agriculture—what he and his colleagues believed in and what the peasantry disliked. Thus, in the Chinese case, power was basically consolidated in the same way it was seized—through "the barrel of a gun." But the seizure of power was facilitated by the introduction of popular reforms in "liberated" areas, (false) promises to those threatened by the revolution, and a delay in the introduction of the full force of socialism until power was truly consolidated.

In Ethiopia the reigning government of Emperor Haile Selassie was not militarily defeated; it was simply ousted in a military coup d'état. The backwardness of Ethiopia contributed to the ease of consolidating power, as did the military's virtual monopoly of the instruments of coercion. Organized opposition to the military came from student organizations, but these were annihilated in the Red Terror of 1977. Arguably, though, the real consolidation of power, and the concurrent "accession of the extremists," came through purges in the military. Given the abruptness of the coup, the military had not developed a plan of government. In the end, moderates advocating compromise were executed, leaving the fanatical Major Mengistu Haile-Mariam as head of state.

> Mengistu, swift and vicious when his power was threatened, struck back.... [D]uring a regular meeting of the Steering Committee of the [Military] Council ... Mengistu and his supporters suddenly left the room, leaving behind the seven men he considered his chief enemies. Mengistu's bodyguards ... entered with machine guns.... Mengistu joined ... [and] together they "executed" them all.... Mengistu was voted Chairman.[9]

During a visit to Moscow in 1978, Mengistu said that the Ethiopian revolution had been historically unique because the army had assumed the vanguard role that was normally reserved for the Communist party.[10] There is an element of truth in Mengistu's claim, but in addition to slighting the important role played by students and intellectuals, he made no acknowledgment of the divisions within the military or the bloody way that accord had been reached.

The Nicaraguan case is perhaps most instructive. The Nicaraguan Revolution was a "social" revolution, based on widespread public opposition and resistance to the Somoza dictatorship. Indeed, the

---

[9] Dawit Wolde Giorgis, *Red Tears* (Trenton, N.J.: Red Sea Press, 1989), p. 29.

[10] Christopher Clapham, *Transformation and Continuity in Revolutionary Ethiopia* (Cambridge: Cambridge University Press, 1988), p. 65.

Sandinistas had no more than twenty-five hundred troops under arms when the dictatorship fell in July 1979. Yet the Sandinista National Liberation Front (FSLN) was able to consolidate power adroitly, and without resort to authoritarian tactics, because of its initiative, the disarming concessions it offered, and the absence of a well-organized alternative source of power, as well as by virtue of its position as the military vanguard of the revolution. The Sandinistas' consolidation of power enabled them to determine the institutional structure of the new government and to define the authority and composition of its organizational units.[11]

The keys to the FSLN's success in consolidating power were its consistent practices of retaining final authority and of delaying the establishment of institutional structures. The institutional structures that eventually emerged were based on the FSLN's unilateral decisions. Concessions were made initially to other political actors, but these were all of the type that could be rescinded. Also, the initial appointment of moderates and conservatives to important government positions undermined the determination and unity of those people who were apprehensive about the aims of the Sandinistas. Once the FSLN had consolidated power, however, these appointed moderates and conservatives were dismissed and replaced.

Seemingly in all cases, revolutionary regimes create a support base for the consolidation of power at the highest levels of government through the establishment and mobilization of new political actors throughout society. Parallel organizations are established to weaken existing organizations (such as trade unions) that are not tied to the government. Threatening organizations are isolated or repressed. Equally important, triumphant revolutionaries create new institutions, often called "mass organizations," where none had existed among the urban and rural poor majority. These government-sponsored organizations are developed and strengthened through ongoing efforts at political suasion and by channeling government services and goods through them.

At the same time that triumphant revolutionaries strengthen their political control, they also consolidate their hold on the military. If the previous regime's military has been defeated, then it is replaced with a military loyal to the interests of the revolutionaries. Irregular guerilla forces are turned into professional armies, a task that often involves weeding out opportunistic rogues. Thus, the Mozambique leader Samora Machel was compelled to give a speech in Maputo titled, "We

[11] Stephen Gorman, "Power and Consolidation in the Nicaraguan Revolution," *Journal of Latin American Studies* 13 (May 1981): 138.

Must Remove the Enemy within the Defence and Security Forces."[12] If, in contrast, the existing military itself is the backbone of the revolution, then the military is purged of those soldiers and officers who are not committed politically to the unfolding of the revolution. In both cases, constant political indoctrination is viewed as essential to ensure that, as one Sandinista put it, the "new" army "knows whose interests it is protecting and who are the enemies of those interests."[13]

As those most committed to radical change within revolutionary coalitions acceded to power, the ambitious ideas that were intellectually fashionable among them were put into practice with the full force available in the respective polities. The shedding of moderates removed constraints. The new governors had considerable freedom of choice in selecting goals and in building those institutions of the state judged most suitable for the pursuit of those ends.

Institutions of Government

In a review of the Soviet Union's foreign policy in the poorer regions of the world, Alvin Rubinstein concluded, "The Soviet Union . . . [was] not a major actor in national liberation struggles."[14] Socialist ideology came to contemporary revolutionary elites principally from their own studies and reflection, much of it in capitalist countries where colonialism provided links of language and culture. What was learned of socialism were devastating critiques of capitalist societies, inspiring political analyses, and visions of a better future for backward societies. Little was learned beforehand of the actual experience of implementing socialism. But when the revolutions triumphed, the example—and sometimes the direct help—of the Soviet Union was often instrumental in providing a blueprint for redesigning the instruments of government. Indeed, Rubinstein concludes that the Soviets' most important assistance to revolutionary regimes was political institution-building.[15] According to him, the Soviets linked the irreversibility of a revolution to institutionalization of political power, more than to economic transformation.[16] "The essential components of the Soviet package . . . [were] a theology of self-legitimation and internal unification, an organizational model for mass control and mobilization, and a security apparatus to nip plots in the bud and eliminate oppo-

---

[12] Barry Munslow, ed.; Michael Wolfers, trans., *Samora Machel*, p. 185.

[13] Quoted in Gorman, "Power and Consolidation," p. 124.

[14] Alvin Rubinstein, *Moscow's Third World Strategy* (Princeton: Princeton University Press, 1988), p. 118.

[15] Ibid., p. 181.

[16] Ibid., p. 180.

sition."[17] This prefabricated structure could institutionalize power and implement desired policies.

In one of the first—and certainly the most consequential—revolutions in the post–World War II period, Soviet advisers played a direct role. From 1949 to 1956, Soviet advisers directed the building of China's new government, which came to emulate openly the government of the Soviet Union. Most prominent was the marriage between the Communist Party and the state. China also came to have Soviet-style economic ministries, a state planning commission, and other structures that ensured the state's control over economic resources.[18] Following, and even extending, the precedent of the Soviet Union, the Chinese Communist Party forced all urban residents to become members of one or more Communist-controlled organizations set up in their workplaces and residential neighborhoods, and it enrolled all workers in Communist-run unions.

Subsequent revolutions often gave rise to unabashed copies of the Soviet and Chinese governmental structures. In the tiny island state of Grenada, even the organization of youth was modeled after the Soviet's Leninist Communist League of Youth.[19] Soviet-style institutions were frequently judged best able to protect revolutionary elites from political challenges and to promote rapid economic development and social transformation. Often the first step was the transformation of the successful revolutionary movement, or in the popular lexicon of the period, the "front," into a Soviet-style Communist party. For example, in South Yemen the National Liberation Front (NLF) transformed itself into a centralized "scientific socialist party," named the Yemeni Socialist Party (YSP).[20] In Angola:

> A new MPLA–Partido do trabalho [worker's party] (MPLA-PT) "guided by the scientific ideology of the proletariat, Marxism-Leninism," emerged.... It assumed a pyramidal shape, from a base of local cells ... on up ... through area, district, and provincial committees to the party congress, its central committee, and finally to the latter's political bureau. The congress confirmed the personal authority of Agostinho Neto as leader of the party and thus of the entire political system.... The MPLA-PT assumed "political, economic and social leadership over the state" and its "efforts to build a socialist society."[21]

[17] Ibid.

[18] Ranbir Vohra, *China* (New Delhi: Penguin, 1990), p. 27.

[19] Paul Seabury and Walter McDougall, eds., *The Grenada Papers* (San Francisco: Institute for Contemporary Studies, 1984), p. 107.

[20] Fred Halliday, *Revolution and Foreign Policy* (Cambridge: Cambridge University Press, 1990), p. 34.

[21] John Marcum, "The People's Republic of Angola," in Edmond Keller and Donald Rothchild, eds., *Afro-Marxist Regimes* (Boulder, Colo.: Lynne Rienner, 1987), p. 72.

As elsewhere, the building of Soviet-style state institutions in Angola was not a spontaneous or public-driven occurrence. It was a deliberate decision made by a small urbane, intellectual, revolutionary elite.

> At the time, few MPLA members were familiar with even the most basic concepts of Marxism-Leninism. They knew little or nothing of dialectical materialism, democratic centralism, or dictatorship of the proletariat. Faced with this reality . . . the MPLA opened a National Party School in Luanda to train political cadres. . . . Unprepared to delay realization of the desired new political order, MPLA leadership decided simply to declare the adherence of thousands of MPLA followers to the pursuit of "scientific socialism" as a given. This adherence was said to be grounded in popular "trust" in the movement and its guide "Comrade President Agostinho Neto."[22]

Despite its own shallowness, the MPLA sought to mobilize and educate Angolans about the "objectives of socialist revolution," a task that was facilitated by the party's control over all news media.

Intellectual fashion and Soviet assistance led to a remarkable similarity among the political institutions of diverse revolutionary regimes. Thus, countries as disparate as Laos and South Yemen adopted the prefix, "The People's Democratic Republic," Burkina Faso and Nicaragua alike had "neighborhood defense committees," and Cuba and Mozambique shared the slogan, "people's power." Across continents, the rhetoric to drum up popular support for revolutionary institutions shared the same phraseology and iconography. In the post–World War II era, there may have been different routes to revolutionary upheaval, but there is a stunning similarity in the political institutions built by triumphant revolutionary elites.

In a few cases, those who ascended to power in the aftermath of a revolution were not steadfastly committed to socialism. Here, the remaking of government did differ and did not culminate in a monolithic state. Although the elite of the Bolivian National Revolutionary Movement (MNR) had formal control as a single-party regime for twelve years, it was unable to structure and contain the energies that surged forth with the revolution. Nasser and his fellow officers in Egypt governed as a military dictatorship under the name of the Revolutionary Command Council (RCC). Nasser's late commitment to socialism (which was never complete) did not result in fundamental changes in the personalistic way he exercised power. The most striking exception, though, was Iran. Clerical domination of the state was written into the constitution and largely realized in practice. The institutions of the government were largely republican, augmented by "revo-

---

[22] Ibid.

lutionary organizations" and a swollen state security apparatus. But what was most novel was the responsibility assigned to the clerics to formulate state ideology, watch over technocrats running ministries, and determine laws.[23]

With these exceptions duly acknowledged, it remains remarkable how those who ascended to power in the aftermath of victory so overwhelmingly modeled their institutions of government after the Soviet Union. It is especially remarkable since they had so little information about the accumulated experience of how well those institutions worked in the Soviet Union, or even how those institutions would translate to settings with different historical, social, and geographical characteristics. This faithful, indeed blind copying is a further testament to the power of ideas in determining political choices.

Policies and Imagined Potency

Contemporary revolutionary regimes have committed themselves to a broad transformation of state and society, leading to efforts to reconfigure government, economy, society, and culture. In some instances, revolutionary regimes have presumed to seek the perfection of human nature, as in the Cuban and Laotian attempts to create a New Socialist Man. In many, the more attainable goals of eradicating illiteracy and reducing gender inequality have been targeted. But in all of the regimes, with the sole exception of Iran, economic goals have been at the very center of their purpose. Even Che Guevara, who was the most ardent proponent of the concept of the New Man in Cuba, stated, "Our primary aim is to give a better standard of living to everyone."[24] Similarly, Fidel Castro commented, "Communism certainly cannot be established if we do not create abundant wealth."[25]

Widespread commitment to the economic ideals of socialism results in a relatively common set of core policies:

1. Elimination of the economic role of foreign capitalists.

2. State expropriation and management of large landed estates and industrial enterprises.

3. Collectivization of agriculture.

4. State control over the direction of the growth of the economy.

---

[23] Shaul Bakhash, *The Reign of the Ayatollahs*, rev. ed. (New York: Basic Books, 1990), p. 291.

[24] Quoted in David Morawetz, "Economic Lessons for Some Small Socialist Developing Countries," *World Development* 8 (May–June 1980): 339.

[25] Ibid., p. 362.

5. Income redistribution.

6. Improvement of the welfare of lower classes through government services and programs (such as health care and food subsidies).

Behind the articulation of these goals is a conviction, fostered by socialist ideology, that extensive state involvement in the economy will produce best results. And what the state itself cannot do is best done by individuals working together cooperatively. The private is replaced with the public. Suggestively, even those revolutionary regimes that were not initially politically committed to socialist ideology and institutions fell under the influence of these prescribed policy choices.

Nationalization often begins immediately with the seizure of power, with the confiscation of both the commanding heights of the economy and the property of the principal enemy (or enemies) of the revolution. Often the two are the same, or nearly so. For example, in Bolivia the nationalization of mining companies eliminated the power of three disliked mining companies and gave the MNR dominant control over the production of the minerals that provided 90 percent of the country's foreign exchange earnings.[26] In Algeria, it was the French-owned oil industry that was promptly nationalized.

The initial wave of nationalization gives the new regime substantial, but incomplete, control over the economy. Still, nationalization is of decisive importance. Even in Iran, the increase in the state's responsibilities is the most consequential change with the emergence of a new, revolutionary regime:

> The revolution led to considerable disruption and to far-reaching changes in the structure of the Iranian economy.... [Most] significantly, the government took over large sectors of the economy through nationalization and expropriation, including banking, insurance, major industry, large-scale agriculture and construction, and an important part of foreign trade. It also involved itself in the domestic distribution of goods. As a result, the economic role of the state was greatly swollen and that of the private sector greatly diminished by the revolution.[27]

This account of the significance of state nationalization generally fits other cases as well.

Variations among countries in the amount and kinds of property nationalized in the initial phase can be ascribed in large measure to the strength of various economic sectors and their relation to the deposed elite. As nationalization continues, more significant and less easily explained differences arise in its extent and pace. In China and Cuba,

---

[26] Walter Gómez, "Bolivia," *Journal of Developing Areas* 10 (July 1976): 461, 474.

[27] Bakhash, *The Reign of the Ayatollahs*, p. 166.

nationalization of the economy continued rapidly: in China it was complete in seven years, and in Cuba nearly so in nine years (thirty percent of the agricultural sector remained the only exception). A notable contrast occurred in such backward countries as Laos, Mozambique, and Ethiopia. Here, nationalizations proceeded at a much slower pace, often only in response to problems arising in individual private enterprises. For example, in Ethiopia—a predominantly agrarian country—never more than five percent of cultivated land was directly held by state farms. However, the Ethiopian revolutionary state controlled agriculture in other ways, particularly through its control of the prices of agricultural inputs and through the forced requisition of harvests.

As attractive as Marxism-Leninism is to revolutionary elites, the doctrine gives government little specific guidance. The Soviet Union, and to a lesser extent China, provided institutional blueprints, but only a limited sense of how newly created institutions were to be administered. Thus, revolutionary regimes inspired by Marxism-Leninism had no guidelines on how to manage, for example, a ministry, a bank, or an enterprise. Marxism-Leninism, as it was understood, also had nothing to say about such mundane but consequential concerns as growth of the money supply, taxation, or income policies.

From an administrative perspective, Marxism-Leninism is more a *mentalité* than a coherent and all-encompassing plan of government. This distinction points to the obscure and unconscious elements in a given worldview. It explains both the millenarian ideas among revolutionary elites and their faith in public institutions (especially the state itself), as well as their ignorance of how these new or at least revamped institutions were to be managed in the pursuit of Herculean transformations. Moreover, without contributing new forms of administration, Marxism-Leninism and the revolutionary process itself discredited and debased traditional management, including accounting, profits, banks—and even a full day's work.

While decisions to employ and extend the state in the management of the economy were inspired by a faith in socialism, they often also were pragmatic responses to pressing problems and threats. The most common problem was the production and requisition of needed goods—food, consumer products, or commodities that earn foreign exchange. Thus, for example, the rapid expansion of state farms in Ethiopia was explained as a means "to meet the growing shortages of grain in the urban areas and the raw material supply of the country's major manufacturing industries."[28] The provision of foodstuffs, espe-

---

[28] Quoted in Forrest Colburn, *Managing the Commanding Heights* (Berkeley: University of California Press, 1990), p. 21.

cially at low cost, and the generation of foreign exchange to pay for imports can be crucial in meeting the consumption needs of those loyal to the revolution, including cadres, and of others whose support is deemed important, such as residents of the capital city.

Similarly, the state may intercede to avoid turning over productive enterprises to either laborers or peasants. The apprehension is not just that economies of scale may be lost, but also that what is produced may be consumed locally, thus disrupting the flow of goods and services to other sectors, including the state itself. Also, access to property and capital—especially if it occurs unequally—may foster social inequities and engender antirevolutionary behavior. The influential Cuban statesman Carlos Rafael Rodríguez concurs in the Leninist view that distributing land to individuals buttresses capitalism: "The small land-holder promotes capitalism, hour by hour, minute by minute."[29]

In sectors of the economy in which the revolutionary state cannot intervene directly, prominently in peasant agriculture, it fosters cooperatives. These cooperatives are perceived as a means of securing rapid agricultural growth, in part because of a belief in the economies of scale but also because cooperation itself is seen as energizing. Revolutionary elites often believe that political challenges can best be met if independent peasants have been incorporated into collective structures. General Secretary Kaysone Phomvihane told a Laotian congress:

> At present the great majority of the peasants in our country are organized under different forms of collective work, ranging from mutual aid teams, solidarity production groups to various types of cooperatives. It is necessary to understand that those labor collectives are not only economic but also political organizations. Therefore, we must try our best to consolidate and heighten the effectiveness of those organizations in mobilizing and educating the peasants, raising their political consciousness, deepening their patriotism and love of socialism, enhancing their tradition of diligent labor, solidarity, mutual love and mutual assistance, thus inspiring them to implement actively the party's and state's policies, to intensify production in order to build up a civilized style of living and the new country-side.[30]

The formation and nurturing of cooperatives is, alongside nationalization, the main vehicle of socialism and social transformation in poor

[29] Carlos Rafael Rodríguez, *Letra con filo*, vol. 2 (Havana: Editorial de Ciencias Sociales, 1983), p. 397.

[30] Grant Evans, *Lao Peasants under Socialism* (New Haven: Yale University Press, 1990), pp. 181–182.

countries. Indeed, the similarity of experience in which millions of peasants were ushered into cooperative forms of agriculture—from China, to Southeast Asia, to Afghanistan, to Ethiopia, to Algeria, to lusophone Africa, to Cuba and Nicaragua—is one of the most stunning indicators of the extent to which revolutionary ideas have shaped lives.

The management of nationalized factories and farms and the promotion of cooperatives are directed by a state that seeks to replace broadly the "anarchy of the market" with "rational planning" and to supplant selfish individual incentives and initiative with social cooperation. Toward these ends, the revolutionary state assumes many new powers and responsibilities, including significant direct or indirect control over any remnants of private economic activity. Thus, foreign trade, banking and insurance, and the setting of prices of domestically traded goods—especially foodstuffs—are administered by newly established bureaucracies. To promote public support of its economic program, and to rally political loyalty, revolutionary states also assume major and sometimes complete responsibility for education, the media, and the arts. In Cuba, for example, even posters are under the jurisdiction of the Party's Committee on Revolutionary Orientation.[31]

Revolutionary zeal encouraged the expectation that these social changes, prominently the reorganization of economic activity, would lead to a spontaneous upsurge of productive activity. Commonly, there were greatly exaggerated beliefs in the potency of these new organizational forms and in their presumed ability to unleash enthusiasm, diligence, creativity, and heroism. There was frequently, too, a conviction that the military discipline and sacrifice that enabled revolutionaries to triumph could be continued in the mundane tasks of economic reconstruction and development. Economic tasks were depicted as being like military offensives and battlefronts. Typically, in Cambodia, renamed Democratic Kampuchea, it was claimed, "Our male and female combatants and people will surely succeed in their determined offensive to build our beloved fatherland by leaps and bounds and make it prosperous."[32] Revolutionary hubris not only shaped many policies, but also leaders' expectations of their potential, which prompted a refusal to retrench when early expectations were confounded.

---

[31] Michael Myerson, *Memories of Underdevelopment* (New York: Grossman, 1973), p. 199.

[32] Quoted in Karl Jackson, "The Ideology of Total Revolution," in Karl Jackson, ed., *Cambodia 1975–1978* (Princeton: Princeton University Press, 1989), p. 62.

Conclusion

In summary, socialism overwhelmingly captivated the political imagination of the revolutionary elites who ascended to power in the aftermath of the overthrow of the old regimes. Often a passionate commitment to socialism was what propelled revolutionaries into power. In every contemporary case of revolution, those few within the revolutionary coalition who ascended to power committed their polity to more than just replacing a government deemed illegitimate. Usually it was socialism as an ideology, or at least as a *mentalité*, that provided a blueprint for building a new, decidedly enlarged, more ambitious state. Concomitantly, socialism suggested a set of bold new policies for the conquest of poverty, inequality, and dependence. The Soviet Union, as an established socialist state, provided a model for, and at times outright assistance in, state-building. Yet revolutionaries had surprisingly little information, from either their own sources or from representatives of the Soviet Union, on how these influential ideas had been working in practice. Thus, efforts at sweeping social transformation in some of the poorest countries of the world were begun with a grandiose institutional model, ambitious policy prescriptions, tremendous enthusiasm, and no validation in experience.

It was common, and eminently reasonable, for revolutionary elites to insist upon adapting socialism to local conditions. There were important variations in the style and tempo according to which the institutions of socialism were built and socialist policies were implemented. These differences are important. Yet what remains astounding is how countries so culturally distinct and so geographically separate had such similar revolutionary programs.

5

Dependency, Administration, and Foot-Dragging

IN THEIR PURSUIT of rapid, broad-based economic development, revolutionary regimes confront many obstacles. First, there is the material and social damage caused by the insurrection. Second, fledgling regimes face opposition and subversion from defeated political forces and from social strata and international actors who perceive themselves threatened by revolutionary change. Resistance to the revolution is often overt, but it is certainly likely to involve also tacit forms of opposition, such as capital flight and withdrawal from production. Finally, material scarcity—poverty—limits the parameters of policy innovation.

These immediate and predictable problems have been compounded by even more complex difficulties, so that an atmosphere of crisis and austerity has become the normal condition of economic policy in the postrevolutionary setting. Rosy expectations are frustrated. While some states, notably Cuba, reduced inequality, economic growth has in most cases been disappointing, and in some cases absent altogether. At the sixth congress of the Vietnamese Communist Party, held in 1986, the opening address was solemn:

> We must see even more clearly the reverse side of the situation, especially concerning the socioeconomic field, with sluggishness in production, confusion in distribution and circulation, difficulties in the people's lives, negative phenomena in several aspects of life and a decline in the working people's confidence.[1]

Vietnam's sorry—and completely unexpected—record is typical. In Nicaragua, for example, a decade of Sandinista rule (and an accompanying counterrevolution) left the country with a per capita income equivalent to what had been attained forty years earlier.

The reasons for the failure of policies spawned by the revolutionary political culture of Marxism-Leninism are multiple and intertwined. I suggest and adumbrate six propositions, which I hold to be decisive in explaining poor regime performance. Other propositions could be

---

[1] Quoted in Michael Williams, *Vietnam at the Crossroads* (London: Pinter, 1992), p. 48.

advanced; these six are important, though not exhaustive. They serve to focus attention on how the ideas that drove contemporary revolutionary elites have been incompatible with the social and material realities of their respective polities.

The case these propositions make is structural. The importance of leadership and decision making is not denied. However, there are profound structural constraints on leadership that arise from the limited public understanding of—and commitment to—socialism, from the fragility of economies, the dependence on trade, the limits to state autonomy and capacity, and the conditioning of political support on economic performance. It is these kinds of constraints that bedevil revolutionary elites and create surprising uniformity in the trajectory and performance of regimes across countries that are otherwise quite different from one another.

Absence of "Class Consciousness"

In the poor countries of the world, revolutions have been fought (and won) not to build socialism or some other idealized society, but to dispose of colonialists or a despot. Strictly speaking, they have not been class revolutions. Typically, the success of the revolution was made possible by cross-class unity. Socialism came later, as a by-product of the revolutions, foisted on the polities by determined political elites. As a consequence, the constellation of forces committed to socialism has been decidedly less than European socialist theory suggests as a requisite. Often initially there is not even a "vanguard party," let alone an informed, unified, and committed alliance of workers and peasants. Indeed, in some cases there is no "proletariat": in Guinea-Bissau, the industrial labor force numbered a mere eighteen hundred, most of whom were under Portuguese control until liberation.[2] With the absence of a "popular" base for the construction of socialism, it has been implemented either through unsustainable populist economic measures, authoritarian tactics, or some combination of the two. The former creates economic problems, and the latter erodes the state's legitimacy.

Given that the initial social bases of support for contemporary revolutions are often narrow, the creation of new political structures to increase, concentrate, and institutionalize power requires the mobilization of broad support. In carrying out this task, elites confront a

---

[2] Crawford Young, *Ideology and Development in Africa* (New Haven: Yale University Press, 1982), p. 29.

number of contradictions and conflicts. On the one hand, assaulting the old order provokes economic disruptions that put potential support groups in economically problematic situations. The need to restore and ultimately increase economic production and investment to attain greater economic development demands that an investable surplus be accumulated, and this need calls for the restriction of local groups' consumption.[3] At the same time, revolutionary leaders often accrue a large debt to their supporters. The revolutionary movement is usually based on support mobilized through slogans expressing previously frustrated demands, so soon after the insurrection has succeeded, there is anticipation of gratification. These points of contradiction result in an ongoing tension between political and economic logics.[4]

Efforts to redistribute wealth and income to those who constitute the largest stratum of the poor are handicapped by the fact that these individuals are often marginal to the rest of the economy. It is difficult to raise the productivity of a population that lacks so many of the productive requisites, such as minimum investment capital, education, and skills.[5] Thus, redistributed resources are invested with but little yield, or are simply consumed. The beneficiaries of redistribution policies may regard their gains as the spoils of victory, and not as capital to be prudently husbanded and made to increase production. The rhetoric of the revolutionary elite often fosters such an attitude.

In China, "immediately after the liberation, the feelings of the masses soared and swelled," and work discipline relaxed.[6] Similarly, many Nicaraguans thought that after the revolution they would suddenly have everything they never had before, and that they would no longer have to work. Hours worked per day fell nearly everywhere, as did production. The Minister of Agricultural Development and Agrarian Reform, Commander of the Revolution, Jaime Wheelock, summarized the problem:

> Since the triumph of the revolution we have observed in the countryside that contracts made by labor organizations with the Ministry of Labor, and in general with productive enterprises, have presented a tendency to set lower norms for work than existed previously. In sugar, the fall has equaled

[3] James Malloy, "Generation of Political Support and Allocation of Costs," in Carmelo Mesa-Lago, ed., *Revolutionary Change in Cuba* (Pittsburgh: University of Pittsburgh Press, 1971), pp. 26–27.

[4] Ibid.

[5] William Ascher, *Scheming for the Poor* (Cambridge: Harvard University Press, 1984), p. 34.

[6] Franz Schurmann, *Ideology and Organization in Communist China*, rev. ed. (Berkeley: University of California Press, 1966), p. 246.

40 percent of the historic norm, in rice 25 percent, in coffee 60 percent, this is to say, a very steep fall in the productivity of labor. What has happened as a consequence of this? Now we need two workers to do what before one did.[7]

The same pattern is reported elsewhere. In a speech, Samora Machel offered a frank critique of the attitude of workers in Mozambique:

> What did we find in your factories? We saw that you produce very little. So we then asked . . . how we can increase productivity? The answer was always the same: it is impossible to raise productivity because in most enterprises there is poor time-keeping, absenteeism, liberalism, a lack of respect for institutions, confusion . . . the result is low productivity.[8]

Machel suggested that much of the problem derived from a mistaken political *mentalité* among laborers. "They abuse the leeway allowed them and when their attention is called to this, they say: 'Colonialism's finished, exploitation's over.' "[9] In the aftermath of revolution, it is difficult to persuade the poor majority not to celebrate the breakdown of traditional authority relations by reducing labor commitments and enjoying the new government's munificence (such as it may be).

Many revolutionary initiatives requiring popular participation have an immediate cost, and only a future and uncertain payoff. The poor majority is often bound by tradition, averse to risk, poorly educated, isolated by geography, and the victim of underdeveloped communication links and poor transportation networks. Far from being an informed, disciplined coalition partner, the poor majority is likely to be confused, skeptical, and hesitant of many policies, including prominently the collectivization of agriculture.

Because of the absence of a public understanding of and commitment to socialism, revolutionary elites must proselytize extensively while concurrently pursuing a flurry of policies, many of them disruptive. Literacy campaigns are pressed into service, as are education and the dissemination of "news." Factories and farms become pulpits. At least some success is normally achieved, but the dislocations associated with revolutionary initiatives stymie the effort to create, as was said in Grenada, "new revolutionary arteries."[10] Inevitably, regimes

[7] Quoted in Forrest Colburn, "Foot Dragging and Other Peasant Responses to the Nicaraguan Revolution," in Forrest Colburn, ed., *Everyday Forms of Peasant Resistance* (Armonk, N.Y.: M. E. Sharpe, 1989), p. 183.

[8] Barry Munslow, ed.; Michael Wolfers, trans., *Samora Machel* (London: Zed Press, 1985), p. 113.

[9] Ibid., p. 117.

[10] Maurice Bishop and Chris Searle, *Grenada* (London: Education Committee for the British-Grenadian Friendship Society, 1981), p. 23.

must buttress their appeals by drawing upon other formidable resources: authority over the spoils (real or imaginary) of government and use of force. Given the enormousness of the task, frequently such measures are relied upon too heavily, causing financial repercussions and compromising an often implicit commitment to democracy. Thus, because of the narrow support for socialist goals in contemporary revolutions, political elites have to strain fragile resources just to begin the transition to socialism or to another desired ideal.

Limits to State Economic Capability

In the aftermath of the seizure of power, the responsibilities of the state swell dramatically. It takes on numerous tasks, including economic management of "the commanding heights." In contemporary revolutionary regimes, though, bureaucracies have, for a host of reasons, only limited managerial capability. Consequently, their costs exceed their benefits (measured in terms of resources expended and received).

How the state manages the economic responsibilities it assumes is important for a number of reasons. First, its responsibilities include key activities, such as those that generate foreign exchange, those that are the most technically sophisticated, and those that provide a crucial service or product either to the populace at large or to other enterprises. Second, the state often devotes considerable—at times disproportionate—attention and resources to its enterprises. Third, state enterprises, especially those in service industries, often have a major impact on the performance of private enterprises. Fourth, and perhaps most important, state enterprises are assumed to be the "vanguard" of the economy—a model of how the economy is to develop in the future.

In the postrevolutionary epoch, it is daunting to manage most enterprises efficiently and profitably. Markets for inputs are disrupted, work norms are held in abeyance, skilled labor is scarce, and markets for finished products or services are either controlled or depressed. Furthermore, the abrupt transition to state ownership inevitably entails some internal disruption and disorganization. Managerial criteria are likely to be ambiguous, incentives are often inadequate, and supervision is typically superficial.

It is the desire for state enterprises to assist in political tasks, though, that makes for an especially intractable economic environment, in which problems are not tackled aggressively. These essentially economic entities are used in numerous ways, some of them conflicting, as political instruments. At the onset, they are used to smash or at least arrest the old order. Concurrently, they are used to propagate desired political values—to identify themselves as the antithesis of the *ancien régime* and as the bearer of a new order. More concretely, state enterprises are strategically located branches of the government that command resources necessary for a panoply of tasks, from providing social services to mustering recruits for political demonstrations, and, in extreme cases, for armies. In this capacity, state enterprises can be used to reward supporters, both tacit and overt, of the revolution. To fulfill these and other political tasks, state enterprises are extremely useful, usually more so than traditional ministries and government agencies.

Yet state enterprises as economic entities are often the most expensive enterprises in impoverished nations. Meeting political objectives entails high costs: not just a direct material cost but also, through a slighting of economic criteria, a significant but less measurable opportunity cost. The combination of an unfavorable economic environment and the burden of political obligations almost universally results in the loss of considerable sums of money, thus posing a burden on the state, and ultimately on the polity. In many instances, these losses are stunning. A representative characterization comes from an Ethiopian government report: "The performance of most enterprises has not been encouraging and . . . their liquidity position is very precarious. Most of these enterprises have sustained huge losses during that period, thus adding to the already large accumulated deficits brought forward from prior periods."[11] In Mozambique, after six years of postrevolutionary rule, the Ministry of Agriculture admitted that not one state farm was profitable.[12] After the same length of rule in Nicaragua, only four state farms (out of 102) were profitable.[13] Cuba's experience suggests that the propensity of state enterprises to generate losses is profound. At the Third Party Congress (celebrated after twenty-seven years of postrevolutionary rule), Fidel Castro publicly bemoaned the unprofitablity of state enterprises, even asserting that their losses had recently increased.[14]

As a result of these financial deficits, this decisive sector is anything but an economic catalyst. Instead of being the "vanguard" of a booming economy, it is invariably a significant drag, its losses contributing to, rather than alleviating, the sad economic performance of contemporary postrevolutionary regimes. Such feeble state enterprises not only

[11] Ministry of State Farms Development (Ethiopia), untitled report (Addis Ababa, 1985, mimeographed), p. 32.

[12] Joseph Hanlon, *Mozambique* (London: Zed Press, 1984), p. 101.

[13] Conversation with officials of the Ministry of Agricultural Development and Agrarian Reform (MIDINRA), February 1985.

[14] *Granma Weekly Review*, 14 December 1986.

contribute directly to economic problems, especially inflation, but also represent an opportunity cost. Scarce resources entrusted to state enterprises might have been more productively employed elsewhere.

The poor financial performance of state enterprises creates political problems, too. First, the public perception that state enterprises are poorly managed and that the state cannot meet its own expectations weakens the legitimacy of the regime. Second, economic problems, by creating inconvenience and hardships for consumers, contribute to political dissatisfaction. Both of these problems affect the populace at large, including the stated beneficiaries of the revolution—the poor and the dispossessed. Finally, the economic losses of state enterprises create tension within state bureaucracies, as stopgap measures (both political and economic) must be found and hurriedly implemented. These efforts not only obstruct the search for long-term solutions, but also create additional problems. In addition, they reinforce the strong tendency for bureaucracies to reproduce themselves.

In those cases where revolutionary elites have allowed private firms and farms to have a role, the state has proved to be a problematic ally in the production of goods and services. In its bid to plan, regulate, and tax, it often unintentionally stymies production by indirectly raising costs, generating uncertainty, and eroding profit margins. At times government intervention in markets is so extensive that it is a misnomer to speak of a "private sector." Ironically, private initiative often thrives when it is completely outside the scope of government regulation, as is smuggling in Burma.

Economic Dependency

Poor countries, especially those that are small, depend heavily on imports; they must also maintain exports at sufficient levels to prevent the disruption of consumption and investment. This pressure complicates the bid to build socialism. It is likely to be exacerbated by the erstwhile monopolization of the export sector by the well-heeled. Inevitably, revolutionary change disrupts exports. Even if states can take over responsibility for the export sector, they commonly find it unfeasible to alter production of the same commodities—often primary products—for export, because it will affect their foreign-exchange position. An unpalatable example was provided by the People's Revolutionary Government of Grenada, which felt it had to continue promoting tourism.[15] Equally significant, given the necessity of remaining

[15] Jay Mandle, *Big Revolution, Small Country* (Lanham, Md.: North-South Publishing, 1985), pp. 27–33.

competitive internationally, the new regime is likely to find it difficult to end undemocratic and even exploitative forms of production and management. The "socialization" of property remains elusive.

Intellectuals enamored with radical change have commonly ignored the economic implications of making revolutions in poor countries. Dependency theory, which argues that the relationship between wealthy and poor countries is exploitative and perpetuates the dominance of the former over the latter, is curiously silent when it comes to the analysis of postrevolutionary regimes' options in the international economic order.[16] While revolutionary elites have often made verbal commitments to break out of the capitalist-dominated world economic order, and to construct an "independent" economy, no country has actually succeeded. Indeed, accumulated evidence suggests that the poorer the country that attempts revolutionary change, the more dependent it becomes on external economies. Poor countries are simply unable to carry out ambitious development programs without a large infusion of foreign assistance.

Even at their zenith, the Soviet Union and its Eastern European allies were unable to provide development assistance on a scale sufficient to meet the voracious needs of the many revolutionary regimes in poor countries. Thus, the need to import, and therefore to export, endures. Consumption and investment depend on maintaining foreign-exchange earnings. If revolutionary regimes happen to be blessed with substantial earnings from mineral wealth (as are Algeria and Iran), they have more latitude. But most postrevolutionary countries remain vulnerable in their dependence on key foreign-exchange earning sectors—regardless of their ownership. This dependence presents a number of vexing limits to state autonomy.

Revolution entails an assault not only on established political elites, but also on economic elites and their activities. Such elites in revolutionary states tend to be concentrated in the more remunerative export sectors, because they are more remunerative. Invariably, turmoil and initial postrevolutionary policies—especially nationalization—have a depressing effect on both the maintenance of capital investment and its rhythm of production. Capital flight, neglect, and outright sabotage by the former elite lead to problems even before the state can assume direct and indirect control of the export generating sectors. In Nicaragua, for example, assets confiscated from Somoza and his associates were so heavily mortgaged that state officials claim they were bought, not confiscated. Furthermore, for a host of predictable reasons, at least initially the newly established regime may find it difficult to manage its

---

[16] I am grateful to Dessalegn Rahmato for this insight.

swollen economic responsibilities—predominantly the administration of state enterprises. Just when there is soaring demand for foreign exchange (to finance the consolidation of state power, to rebuild capital stocks and inventories from the insurrection, to invest, to expand public services, and to meet the immediate needs of the poor), there is a fall in foreign-exchange earnings. Invariably, this puts a damaging and sometimes embarrassing crimp in government plans and policies.

There is no escaping the need to generate export earnings. To attempt to rupture dependence on traditional export commodities, usually primary products, is conceivable, but Cuba's experience suggests this is fraught with difficulties. Sugar production was despised by the revolutionary elite there because of the low and fluctuating prices it earned, because it offered only seasonal and demeaning employment, and because it led to neither industrialization nor a diversified economy. But the celebrated bid to reduce its importance proved too costly, and ultimately ineffective. Sugar's status on the island has not changed since the revolution; it still provides three-quarters of Cuba's foreign-exchange earnings.[17]

Continued dependence on traditional forms of export generation is all the more frustrating because managerial difficulties and the necessity of remaining competitive internationally impede the "socialization" of property, and often the improvement of workers' real income. These constraints are especially pronounced with such labor-intensive primary products as coffee. Cuba is a notable exception, showing that it is possible to improve workers' standard of living in competitive export sectors, but this success could be achieved only with large subsidies. The inability to escape dependence on traditional and low-yielding activities, and even to alter how work is done and compensated, can lead to disaffection and cynicism among peasants and workers.

Contradictions in Revolutionary Equality

Despite a professed commitment to radical change, revolutionary regimes find it difficult not to allocate resources disproportionately to those sectors that are most important economically and politically. Doing otherwise engenders significant economic problems and instability. Yet the abandonment of well-publicized egalitarian aspirations is politically untenable.

---

[17] Carmelo Mesa-Lago, *The Economy of Socialist Cuba* (Albuquerque: University of New Mexico Press, 1981), pp. 57–65; Medea Benjamin, "Things Fall Apart," *NACLA* 24 (August 1990): 21.

Just as poor countries are highly stratified, government attention and resource allocation are also stratified. Typically, for example, the "modern" or "formal" sector receives priority over the "traditional" or "informal" sector. Industry is favored over agriculture, as is the capital city over the provinces. Politically, those actors most capable of either defending or obstructing the government, such as the military, receive preferential treatment.

Contemporary revolutionary elites are committed to ending stratification through the exercise of state power. This commitment is strong among both those elites who are most enamored with socialism, and those who have a more disparate political imagination (as in the cases of Bolivia, Egypt, and Iran). Ending social stratification entails breaking down structures that defend and reinforce social divisions. At the same time, though, postrevolutionary regimes must maintain existing institutions, be they factories, hospitals, or schools. Recurrent costs, including those for salaried employees, are likely to absorb budgets almost completely, leaving little for new investment. The maintenance of prevailing expenditure patterns is further reinforced by the need to preserve production of important goods and services and to satisfy the consumption needs of the most important political actors.

Efforts to generate new sources of capital and, more important, to empower the poor through the creation of mass organizations, do have some effect. There is likely to be change in the ownership of economic enterprises through nationalization and the recomposition of such political actors as the military. These changes can be significant, ending the abuse of privilege and the usurpation of wealth, at the same time that they open up opportunities for the previously marginalized. However, many established economic and political actors retain their strength. Consequential political and economic entities—from plantations and factories to bureaucracies—are likely still to stand apart from the rest of the economy and polity, and to command a disproportionate amount of resources.

The necessity of maintaining, or more likely restoring, export earnings is an especially compelling impetus for allocating resources in a manner at odds with revolutionary rhetoric. Commandeered resources are directed to where they can be most productive, not to where they are most needed. This allocation holds true for credit, imports (from fertilizers to machinery), and the attention of technicians and bureaucrats. Thus, in Mozambique, pressure to increase food production led the government to allocate considerable funding to the state farms formerly owned by the Portuguese settlers. This policy was perceived as being the easiest and quickest way to increase production. Concomitantly, communal villages, where the bulk of the rural

populace lived and where poverty was most acute, received few resources.[18] In Nicaragua, a persistent shortage of foreign exchange
prompted the Sandinista regime to offer financial incentives, including
dollars disbursed in cash, to the hated but crucial traditional agro-ex-
port elite.[19] There is an economic logic to the allocation of resources
where they can best and most quickly contribute to economic production. But this strategy is politically inconsistent, and harkens back to
the *ancien régime*, where the strong were inevitably favored and the
weak ignored.

There is a tension between revolutionary aspirations and political
and economic imperatives. The more militant the revolution, the more
likely it is to be caught between plummeting economic output and
surging expectations. As a result, either the leadership compromises
itself or it permits the economy to fall to politically dangerous levels.
Like most dilemmas, this one is never neatly resolved.

The Agrarian Question

The weakest parts of socialist theory and practice are the "agrarian
question" and, more particularly, the "peasant problem." In poor
countries, peasants often compose either a substantial part of the population, as in Nicaragua, or an absolute majority, as in Laos. Peasants
are, from a class perspective, the most deserving of support, and indeed this is a supposed pillar of socialist policy. Yet, peasants invariably cling to individualist norms and behavior. Efforts by the regime
to change this behavior often only exacerbate the "stubbornness" of
the peasantry, because the state's bureaucracies are clumsy, and because the state concurrently feels compelled to tax the peasantry.

There is now a wealth of evidence showing socialist agrarian policies to be, in most cases, disappointing, even dismal. Land reform,
often the first act of social reform, favors the peasantry, but subsequent
rural policies, which include collectivization, are often accepted by
rural producers only with great reluctance and resentment. Often
agrarian policy has included agricultural price controls, state requisition of harvests, and restrictions on the free movement of the rural
population. All too often these measures create an atmosphere that
saps peasant initiative and generates dissatisfaction among the very
class that revolutionary elites claim as the backbone of the revolution.

[18] Allen Isaacman and Barbara Isaacman, *Mozambique* (Boulder, Colo.: Westview
Press, 1983), pp. 148–157.
[19] Forrest Colburn, *Post-Revolutionary Nicaragua* (Berkeley: University of California
Press, 1986), pp. 45–61.

Elites, invariably of urban origin and urban-based, fail to acknowledge the breadth of the gap between peasant aspirations and their own collectivist values. Attempts to bridge this gap lead to undesirable consequences.

State bureaucracies in rural areas are commonly insensitive to the needs and aspirations of the rural population. Government policies are often implemented without sufficient preparation of and consultation with the local populace. Reform measures that should merit careful planning and a prolonged gestation period are carried out instead in a rush, often by means of forceful or undemocratic methods. Also, local officials of the state bureaucracies may become zealous advocates of collectivization to please higher authorities and to improve their chances for promotion. Too often, local policies ignore valued rural practices and go against peasant experience. State bureaucrats imagine themselves to be the source of all knowledge, and treat peasant expertise (acquired through generations of experience) as irrelevant.

Equally important, postrevolutionary regimes frequently have insufficient material resources to induce peasants to alter their behavior, offsetting the immediate costs of change. Peasants are conscious, rational decision-makers, and discernible benefits must be provided if they are to change their behavior—be it by joining cooperatives, adopting agricultural innovations, or accepting political mobilization. Benefits must be perceived as benefits; among other factors, that involves consideration of the time horizon and the risk involved.

Not only do postrevolutionary regimes usually lack the skill or resources to induce peasants to relinquish entrenched norms and behaviors, but invariably they tax the peasantry, often heavily. This taxation may not be a preferred course by the regime, but it is likely to be structurally unavoidable. The dilemma is that while poverty is most acute in rural areas, where agriculture is the main livelihood, it is the agricultural sector that produces the two things most important for a poor state—food and export earnings. In an attempt to ensure the well-being (as well as the political support) of urban dwellers, regimes often control food prices. But low food prices for consumers mean low income for farmers. Concurrently, state monopolization of the profits of agricultural exports, often accomplished through a combination of monopsonies and an overvalued exchange rate, likewise will depress rural incomes. The deleterious political effect of state taxation on the agricultural sector is often compounded by the coupling of new social and economic organization, such as the formation of cooperatives, with taxation.

The tragic experience of China is illustrative. Collectivization of agriculture began with the establishment of cooperatives and culminated with a decision In 1958 to make the establishment of communes mandatory.[20] The disruptions engendered by collectivization were sorely aggravated by taxes.

> As China's investment in industry rose . . . grain exports to the Soviet Union were also increased to pay for more heavy machinery. The average amount of grain available to each person in China's countryside . . . dropped to a disastrous 183 kilos in 1959, and a catastrophic 156 kilos in 1960. In 1961 it fell again—to 154 kilos. The result was famine on a gigantic scale, a famine that claimed 20 million lives or more between 1959 and 1962. Many others died shortly thereafter . . . especially children, weakened by years of progressive malnutrition. In the China of 1957, before the Great Leap [Forward] began, the median age of those dying was 17.6 years; in 1963 it was down to 9.7. Half of those dying in China that year . . . were under ten years old.[21]

Sadly, even though food was being produced in rural China, starvation was most pronounced in rural areas.[22] The magnitude of suffering in China is unparalleled. A comparative study by Frederic Pryor identifies the collectivization of agriculture throughout the world as "one of the largest social experiments in history."[23]

Economic Performance and Political Support

The promises of revolutionaries are both economic and political. Yet for the reasons adumbrated, some of which are entirely beyond the fault or control of the new governors, there is likely to be an initial economic reverse, and the first—and formative—years of postrevolutionary rule are likely to be years of economic hardship. Not one exception to this unfortunate (and unforeseen) fate exists. In the midst of economic dislocation, it is difficult to persuade individuals to change their behavior, especially if, as is often the case, the change involves short-term cost and unclear future payoff. An economically besieged government does not have the resources to coax people into abandoning customs or to ensure the productivity of new forms of organizing work. Indeed, economic problems are likely to spawn a host of anti-regime activities: hoarding, speculation, capital flight, and theft. Gen-

[20] Ranbir Vohra, *China* (New Delhi: Penguin, 1990), p. 54.

[21] Jonathan Spence, *The Search for Modern China* (New York: W. W. Norton, 1990), p. 583.

[22] State Statistics Bureau, *Statistical Yearbook of PRC* (Beijing: State Statistics Bureau, 1991), p. 79.

[23] Frederic Pryor, *The Red and the Green* (Princeton: Princeton University Press, 1992), p. 356.

eral support for the government is likely to wane, giving way to doubt and cynicism.

In addition to their own formidable economic difficulties, every contemporary revolutionary regime has been attacked, by either a counterrevolution, a secessionist movement, or an invading neighbor. Whatever their original inspiration may have been, instigators of such opposition attempt to capitalize on economic dislocations and reverses within the revolutionary nation. The cost of defense, whether it be in Mozambique, Burma, or Nicaragua, becomes exorbitant: a drain on resources that could be productively employed, not only in their own right but also as catalysts to stimulate the reshaping of the economy. And since defense of national sovereignty does not necessarily make the populace willing to accept economic change or sacrifice, counterrevolutionary aggression has a political as well as an economic cost.

Postrevolutionary leaders must confront the expectations raised during the insurrectionary period. The inevitable presence of counterrevolutionaries eager to exploit popular discontent makes the challenge all the more pressing. The dangerous temptation in the midst of economic difficulties is to resort to force, the *ultima ratio* of state power. The economic problems and contradictions that confront postrevolutionary regimes, and the political pressures these economic problems bring, help to explain why at least some regimes become less democratic than intended. Economic difficulties also help explain why some postrevolutionary regimes become dependent on international assistance, despite their professed commitment to national autonomy.

Conclusion

The six propositions enumerated clarify why the performance of contemporary revolutionary regimes has been so unsatisfactory. The haunting view that emerges is of revolutionary elites with ambitious plans, but without broad social consensus or adequate resources, yet having an ideologically sustained drive to proceed apace. At times it appears that revolutionaries are buoyed up excessively by the self-confidence gained from successfully overthrowing the *ancien régime*. However, the individual allegiances and class unity mustered for that task are not sustained in the bid to build highly idealized societies. Openly declared or not, cleavages emerge. The intellectually fashionable development strategy—socialism—was expected to unleash resources previously monopolized by former rulers. Yet accumulated evidence suggests that revolution brings no cornucopia of resources to tackle the daunting problems of poor countries.

Revolution may bring existing resources under state control, but that does not translate into an increase in resources. In fact, there are likely to be fewer resources available; at least initially, fungible capital flees and production is disrupted. Management talent is scarce. Limits to state capability prove as detrimental as limits to state autonomy and sheer poverty. Obversely, revolution leads to an explosion of demand for resources by the previously disenfranchised and by the state itself. Given the resulting imbalance, economic crisis is inevitable. More often than not, temporary palliatives—both political and economic—only exacerbate tensions and difficulties.

The brutal confrontation of dreams with intractable political and, especially, economic realities well explains the dispiriting outcomes of contemporary revolutions. Less measurable but sometimes important, too, have been shortcomings—or lapses—in stewardship. The performance of all powerful leaders has in some instances been marred by such personal weaknesses as jealousy and vanity. In other instances, elites have been tempted by the opportunities for corruption facilitated by the centralization of political institutions. And in many cases, political fervor has led to savage intolerance and a resulting disrespect for basic human rights. Fashionable revolutionary discourse has not only been out of touch with economic realities, but has also slighted the inevitable failings of human nature.

The inability of contemporary postrevolutionary regimes to provide much material improvement does not necessarily mean the revolutions should not have been carried out. Just as Marx wrote that the French Revolution cleared away lots of "medieval rubbish," so have recent revolutions in developing countries cleared away many colonial or neocolonial relics. These relics were often not only despotic and unjust, but they were also pervasive obstacles to broad-based development. But the story of contemporary revolutions is a story of revolutionary elites determined to do much more than oust colonialists or dictators. Politically intoxicated, these revolutionaries have shoved their poor societies into an unsustainable recasting of state and economy that has left the majority of people disoriented, politically cynical, and materially more impoverished.

6

War

REVOLUTIONS are often facilitated by war. War weakens and sometimes even destroys regimes. Command of a victorious army provides revolutionaries with easy access to political power, though deftness is often necessary to consolidate power. Many contemporary revolutions have been ushered in by wars: China, Korea, Vietnam, Laos, Cambodia, Algeria, Guinea-Bissau, Angola, and Mozambique.

War is not only a friend of revolutionaries; it can be an enemy too. War often plagues triumphant revolutionaries. The Napoleonic Wars ensued from the French Revolution. Scarcely had Russia made peace with Germany, ending its participation in World War I, than intervention began from countries that Lenin called "the imperialist bandits." For two and a half years, Russia was in a state of undeclared war with Great Britain, France, the United States, and Japan.[1] The shadowing of revolution by war can be traced to increased "levels of threat" between a new revolutionary regime and countries startled by its emergence.[2] Revolution brings a shift in the balance of power, which is difficult to measure and so invites miscalculation: "Revolutions make war more likely by increasing perceptions of threat on both sides and by encouraging both sides to believe that the threat will be easy to defeat."[3] Governors' perceptions of threat may well be mistaken, in which case resulting wars are more the outcome of erroneous perceptions than of actual danger.

Contemporary revolutions have not been spared from war. At least three recent wars originated with such shifts in the balance of power and perceptions of threat: in the aftermath of the Iranian Revolution, the Iraqi leadership concluded mistakenly that Iran was weak, and attacked it to seize territory. The war between Ethiopia and Somalia had similar origins. China attacked Vietnam in 1979 after the Vietnamese invasion of Cambodia because China felt threatened by Vietnam's potential domination of Southeast Asia. Thus, contemporary interstate behavior has not differed appreciably from historical cases.

[1] E. H. Carr, *The Bolshevik Revolution* (Harmondsworth, Middlesex, England: Penguin, 1966), pp. 67, 96–97.

[2] Stephen Walt, "Revolution and War," *World Politics* 44 (April 1992): 322–323.

[3] Ibid., p. 333.

TABLE 2
Revolutions and Ensuing Wars
1945–1990

Revolution	War
Afghanistan	Counterrevolution/civil war
Angola	Civil war
Burma	Ethnic secession movements
Cambodia	Vietnam invasion (1979); ensuing civil war
China	Korean War (1950); Vietnam (1979)
Cuba	Bay of Pigs invasion (1961)
Egypt	Suez Canal crisis (1956)
Ethiopia	Somalia (1977); ethnic secession movements
Grenada	U.S. invasion (1983)
Iran	Iraq (1980)
Mozambique	Counterrevolution/civil war
Nicaragua	Counterrevolution/civil war
North Korea	Korean War (1950)
South Yemen	Border conflicts with North Yemen and Saudi Arabia
Vietnam	France; United States; Cambodia (1979); China (1979)

Note: Dates are given for conflicts that began or occurred at a discrete time.

Four characteristics of contemporary revolutions deserve to be highlighted: (1) "warfare" was not restricted to the classical definition of war—that is, conflict among states—but instead included protracted civil wars; (2) as the countries in which revolutions took place were poor, and often small, they were weaker participants in the international system and suffered from conflict among the "superpowers"; (3) despite ample historical evidence, revolutionary elites have appeared initially oblivious to the international and domestic contention unleashed by revolution; and (4) revolutionary policies often have engendered such resentment that counterrevolutionaries and secessionists found much support. The wars engaged in by the many revolutionary regimes between 1945 and 1990 were not without precedent, but what was notable—and tragic—was the diversity and complexity of the conflicts, and the ways in which the international system and fashionable revolutionary postures and initiatives aggravated conflicts.

Table 2 details the subsequent conflicts that besieged some of the twenty-two countries judged to have experienced a revolution in the post–World War II epoch. The conflicts can be disaggregated into wars proper (interstate conflicts), counterrevolutions, civil wars, and ethnic secessionist insurgencies. These categories, though, are not always discreet. What may begin as a counterrevolution, with the specific intent of rolling back a revolution, may degenerate into a civil war in which the aims of participants are muddled. Factions in civil wars may be based on ethnic cleavages even though there is no consideration by any faction of secession. And ethnic secession movements may gather momentum because of counterrevolutionary sentiment. It is a challenge to unravel the conflicts that have tormented contemporary revolutionary regimes.

The longest conventional war of the twentiety century was the eight-year war between Iran and Iraq. The loss of life in this conflict was staggering: the number of deaths on the two sides exceeded one million, including over 700,000 Iranians. Although the war formally began with the Iraqi invasion of Iran in September 1980, the origins of the conflict can be traced to the Iranian Revolution of the previous year. Throughout the Persian Gulf, that revolution generated a dangerous mixture of intense but vague ambitions, fears, threats, and sense of opportunities.

From the time he acceded to power, the Ayatollah Khomaini vowed to spread the Iranian Revolution throughout the Persian Gulf. In a public address, for example, he bluntly said, "We should export our revolution to other countries of the world and should reject this idea that the revolution should stay within our own borders."[4] Of the Persian Gulf regimes targeted by Khomaini, Iraq was threatened most frequently. Hostile rhetoric was taken especially seriously by the Iraqi leadership because of Iraq's border with Iran and because 55 percent of Iraqis were Shiite Muslims. Iraqi president Saddam Hussein and his cohorts undoubtedly feared that Khomaini, who had succeeded in mobilizing millions of Iranian Shiites against the secular regime of the Shah, might likewise succeed in mobilizing Iraqi Shiites against Hussein's own secular regime.

In addition to presenting a threat, the Iranian Revolution also appeared to offer an opportunity to the Iraqi leadership. In the months following its revolution, Iran suffered from military and economic decline, and social unrest. The Khomaini regime purged between 30 and 50 percent of the country's military officers, slashed the military budget, and canceled orders for military equipment, all of which markedly decreased the fighting capacity and morale of the armed forces.[5] Iran's determination to spread its Islamic revolution led to diplomatic isolation. In contrast, Iraq's leadership believed it could count on the support of countries antagonized by Khomaini.

[4] Behrouz Souresrafil, *The Iran-Iraq War* (Plainview, N.Y.: Guinan, 1989), p. 32.

[5] Shahram Chubin and Charles Tripp, *Iran and Iraq at War* (London: I. B. Tauris, 1988), p. 33.

Although Iraq initiated the war, once begun it was welcomed by the Iranian revolutionary elite, who used it to unite the country under the banner of Islam and patriotism. Khomaini presented the war as Iran's divine duty:

> Had the Prophet come and sat in the Medina mosque all his life just to preach the Koran, then we would have followed him as an example. But he came and from the start of his mission in Mecca he began a struggle. He set up a government; we should do the same. He participated in various wars, we too should fight. He defended [Islam], we too should also defend [it].[6]

The existence of a concrete "enemy" and "threat" to the country gave the leadership a powerful rationale to repress domestic opposition and to cajole society into supporting revolutionary initiatives and government policies. For example, striking bus drivers were scolded by Khomaini: "While our youth are being killed on the war front, you bus drivers are demanding an increase in your wages and are adding to the problems of the government."[7] The bus drivers were filled with remorse and called off their strike. Eventually, by successfully resisting and then expelling the Iraqi invaders, the Iranian government consolidated its Islamic revolution.

The war between Ethiopia and Somalia in 1977–1978 has many parallels to the Persian Gulf conflict. Like Iran and Iraq, Ethiopia and Somalia are historic rivals. And similarly, the aggressor state— Somalia—sought to take advantage of a country weakened by revolution. Ethnic secession movements, counterrevolutionary activity, and civil unrest flourished in most Ethiopian provinces. The military, weakened by purges, was spread thinly throughout the country. The leadership of Somalia believed it could prevail by committing its entire military to the conquest of the Ogaden desert, which it maintained was rightfully part of Somalia. The political elite of Somalia were also confident that the Ethiopian Revolution had shifted international alliances in its favor. The United States had suspended military aid to Ethiopia and was seeking a rapprochement with Somalia. Ethiopia had yet to develop a relationship with the Soviet Union and Cuba.

As happened in Iran, the Ethiopian Revolution elite used the invasion to thwart challenges to its authority. Ethiopians were asked to close ranks, not for the defense of the revolution but out of patriotism. The war thus helped Mengistu consolidate his rule (except in the northern province of Eritrea). Still, the defeat of the Somalians was

---

[6] Quoted in Ibid., p. 41.
[7] Quoted in Behrouz Souresrafil, *The Iran-Iraq War*, p. 123.

ensured only through the support of more than 11,000 Cuban and 1,000 Soviet military personnel and huge Soviet air and sea lifts of arms to beleaguered Ethiopia.[8]

The triangle of conflict among China, Vietnam, and Cambodia in the late 1970s is also traceable to perceived shifts in the balance of power and to resulting threats. The conflicts are notable because they occurred among three revolutionary states, all committed to the same revolutionary ideology—Marxism-Leninism. But ideology did not dissipate national rivalry:

> The real roots of the conflict must be sought in the complicated relationships between China and Vietnam and between Vietnam and Cambodia. Phnom Penh, Hanoi, and Beijing all based their actions on the conviction that their larger adversary was determined to reassert its past dominance over its weaker neighbor. In all cases, that conviction was based to a considerable degree on historical experience. The Pol Pot regime was almost irrational in its fear . . . of Vietnam's historical determination to realize the total submission and even the cultural extinction of the Cambodian state. Hanoi, in turn, appeared convinced that the primary goal of Chinese foreign policy was to reassert its traditional political and cultural domination over Indochina. For its part, China charged that Hanoi's actions in Indochina were a mask for Soviet designs to achieve hegemony in Asia.[9]

In sum, Cambodians did not trust the Vietnamese, the Vietnamese did not trust the Chinese, and the Chinese did not trust the Vietnamese.

Even during their struggle for power, the Cambodian Khmer Rouge regarded the Vietnamese as "Enemy Number One."[10] Following the Cambodian Revolution, all resident Vietnamese were expelled (just as the Vietnamese expelled Chinese). The approximately 4,000 Vietnamese troops in the Cambodian army were purged, with some even executed, in an effort to "purify" the military.[11] Confident of their military abilities following their seizure of power, the Khmer Rouge claimed territories in the Mekong delta area that had been lost to Vietnam long before, and vowed to recover such territories.[12] Border clashes with Vietnam were common.

---

[8] Edmond Keller, *Revolutionary Ethiopia* (Bloomington: Indiana University Press, 1988), p. 206.

[9] William Duiker, *China and Vietnam* (Institute of East Asian Studies, University of California, Berkeley, 1986), pp. 92–93.

[10] King Chen, *China's War with Vietnam, 1979* (Stanford: Hoover Institution Press, 1987), p. 32.

[11] Ibid., p. 33.

[12] Chang Pao-Min, *Kampuchea between China and Vietnam* (Kent Ridge: Singapore University Press, 1985), pp. 42–43.

The rhetoric of the Cambodian revolutionary elite and the behavior of its military were interpreted in Hanoi as attempts by China to bully Vietnam. Thus, a 1978 Vietnamese editorial claimed: "The reactionary Pol Pot–Ieng Sary clique is . . . badly needed by Chinese authorities to carry out their expansionist policy in Indochina and in all Southeast Asia. The Chinese authorities are using . . . [Cambodia] as a tool to oppose Vietnam."[13] Chinese military aid, in fact, did facilitate the nearly doubling of the Cambodian armed forces between 1975 and 1977. Vietnam's successful invasion of Cambodia in 1979 toppled the regime of Pol Pot.

Chinese leaders felt threatened by Vietnam's invasion of Cambodia. The Vietnamese were suspected of attempting to rig an Indochina federation, with Vietnam at its head. And the Chinese leadership saw Soviet designs behind the invasion. Moscow, the principal source of Vietnam's weapons, was perceived as wanting to gain power over all of Southeast Asia through Vietnamese surrogates. Vietnam, in contrast, saw its relationship with the Soviet Union as defensive: Hanoi claimed to have established close relations with Moscow because of suspicion of Chinese intentions, and because it saw a close relationship with Moscow as a way of escaping dependence on China.

In 1979 Chinese troops invaded Vietnam. Although the Vietnamese halted the incursion, casualties were high. Formally, the war lasted a mere seventeen days, but border clashes continued for a decade. This conflict was yet another example of the perilous attachment of war with revolution, illustrating that while revolution may be heralded by euphoria and utopian visions, contemporary revolutionary regimes, like their precursors, have been vulnerable to the greatest bane of states—war with other states.

Counterrevolutions, Civil Wars, and Ethnic Secession

Contemporary revolutionary regimes have not only been embroiled in conflict with threatened or opportunistic neighbors; frequently, they have been beset by counterrevolution, torn apart by civil war, or racked by ethnic secession movements. In the worst cases, such as those in Angola, Mozambique, Ethiopia, and Afghanistan, conflict became so widespread and complicated that it grew difficult to distinguish the motivations and intentions of the contending factions. Furthermore, while the sources of conflict were autochthonous, the Cold War between the United States and the Soviet Union often led to

[13] Quoted in Chen, *China's War with Vietnam*, p. 35.

foreign intervention in the conflicts. The provision of weaponry alone was enough to make these conflicts more costly than would have been the case otherwise.

In Angola, three independence movements, operating in different parts of the country, opposed Portuguese rule. In 1975, when the Portuguese withdrew from the besieged capital of Luanda, the People's Movement for the Liberation of Angola (MPLA) declared itself the sole political successor and proclaimed the creation of the People's Republic of Angola. South Africa intervened on the side of MPLA's rivals, especially the National Union for the Total Independence of Angola (UNITA), which was based in southern Angola. Cuba dispatched 18,000 troops in support of the MPLA. Equipped with Soviet armored vehicles and rocket launchers, these troops were decisive in consolidating the authority of the MPLA. The National Front for the Liberation of Angola (FNLA), the third of the revolutionary forces, was virtually annihilated in the north of the country. However, the confrontation with UNITA settled into an intractable civil war: with the backing of the United States, the UNITA rebels dominated much of the countryside, while the MPLA government, supported by up to 50,000 Cuban troops and extensive Soviet aid, controlled most urban areas.[14]

The civil war was fueled not only by foreign intervention, but also by the new regime's ideological rigidity. Given its mostly urban origins, Portuguese schooling, and high proportion of *mestiço* leadership, the MPLA had difficulty in relating effectively to the overwhelming majority of Angolans, who were ill-educated, rural, and black. But it was the MPLA's zealotry and intolerance that were fatal; the MPLA declared itself a Marxist-Leninist party with absolute control over the press, the economy, and the state, and it conferred upon itself the right to reshape society. Its strident campaigns against organized religion generated hostility. Rejecting the local importance of ethnicity, the MPLA refused to make efforts to bring underrepresented ethnic groups into the top ranks of party leadership. All important agricultural policies were modeled on Soviet experience—centralization, mechanization, and collectivization—to the neglect of peasant needs and opinions.[15] Despite its brutality, UNITA was able to recruit Angolans to oppose the ensconced MPLA government.

In 1988, after years of fighting, the death of hundreds of thousands of Angolans, and the wrecking of the country's economy and social infrastructure, international agreement was reached for curtailment of

[14] Arthur Banks, ed., *Political Handbook of the World* (Binghamton, N.Y.: CSA Publications, 1991), p. 21.

[15] John Marcum, "The People's Republic of Angola," in Edmond Keller and Donald Rothchild, eds., *Afro-Marxist Regimes* (Boulder, Colo.: Lynne Rienner, 1987), pp. 74–76.

foreign military involvement. But domestic reconciliation proved more difficult and fighting has continued.

In Mozambique, conflict had its origin in the formation of the Mozambique National Resistance (RENAMO or MNR) by the white-minority-ruled Rhodesian government. Supposedly, RENAMO's original intent was to gather intelligence, but following the transformation of Rhodesia into Zimbabwe in 1980, RENAMO developed into a counterrevolutionary organization. With military aid from South Africa, it committed terrorism and sabotage in all of Mozambique's ten provinces. Support was obtained in part through terror and coercion, but also in part by virtue of peasant dissatisfaction with the Marxist government policies. As in other cases, the collectivization of agriculture in particular engendered widespread resentment and resistance.[16] The governor of one province acknowledged: "All peasants are individualistic. At first sight they think that all collective life must be bad. The resistance has built on this, encouraging people to live in the traditional way. It promotes tribal differences. . . . In rural areas many families have at least one member fighting for MNR."[17] What is difficult to explain in Mozambique is the savagery of the fighting, which has commonly included the execution and mutilation of women and children by counterrevolutionary forces.

Just as tragic as the southern African cases of Angola and Mozambique is the case in Afghanistan, another of the world's poorest countries. The country encompasses a multitude of ethnic groups and languages, and a raft of religious factions. Mountains isolate many regions and cultures, breeding a fierce sense of independence and a fear of encroachment upon perceived natural rights. The 1978 revolution had a narrow social base, and subsequent revolutionary initiatives spawned bitter resistance. Although such reforms as land redistribution, championing of women's rights, and annulment of farmers' debts were "progressive" in appearance, they upset deeply ingrained economic and cultural practices. Furthermore, these reforms were often hastily and ineptly executed.[18]

Several counterrevolutionary movements emerged. The Soviet Union felt compelled to offer military support to the fledgling "socialist" regime. An initial airlift of 4,000 troops in 1979 grew to a force of more than 110,000 by mid-1982. But the presence of Soviet troops only

---

[16] Alex Vines, *Renamo* (Centre for Southern African Studies, University of York, York, England, 1991), pp. 1, 2, 114–117.

[17] Quoted in Ibid., p. 117.

[18] *New York Times*, 30 April 1992; Jan-Heeren Grevemeyer, "Modernisation from Below," in Bol Huldt and Erland Jansson, eds., *The Tragedy of Afghanistan* (London: Croom Helm, 1988), pp. 122, 132–133.

fueled armed resistance, which came to be directed as much toward ousting "foreign invaders" as toward the toppling of an unpopular regime, both of which were judged anti-Islamic.

To check what was viewed as Soviet expansionism, the United States funneled enormous quantities of military aid to the *mujaheddin* (warriors of the Holy War), who were active throughout the country but organized only at the local level. Soviet troops left nine years later, although fighting between the revolutionary government and the *mujaheddin* continued until the government fell in 1992. A million Afghans were killed in the civil war, and somewhere around five million Afghans—a fourth of the population—were forced to flee to western Pakistan or northern Iran.[19]

A different kind of conflict, but one just as tragic, took place in Ethiopia and continues in Burma—ethnic insurgency. In both countries, ethnic conflict antedates efforts at revolutionary change: the rebellion of the Karens (the largest of many minority groups) in Burma dates back to 1949, and the Eritrean struggle for nationhood is traced to 1961.[20] Indeed, the inability to resolve ethnic conflict was one of the factors that led to military coups in Burma and Ethiopia, coups which, in turn, resulted in radical attempts to remake society. But the socialist model that was adopted only fueled these rebellions. A summary of the Burmese case is instructive:

> Ne Win . . . [was] encouraged . . . to believe that . . . a military government unfettered by civilian restrictions could solve this intractable problem [of ethnic insurgencies] once for all. In fact nothing was further from the truth. Ironically the 1962 coup gave many of the insurgencies a new lease of life. Ne Win's thinly disguised Burmanisation policies and attempt to create a submissive one-party state in a country of such obvious ethnic and cultural diversity pushed many hitherto little affected sections of the community into the insurgents' camp. But it was above all his extraordinary Burmese Way to Socialism and attempt to build a reconstructed socialist economy, isolated from the outside world, which was to prove his undoing.[21]

Burma's twenty-five insurgent groups, most comprising ethnic-minority armies, operate in or loosely control one-quarter of Burma.[22] There has been considerable loss of life and a squandering of sorely needed resources.

[19] *New York Times*, 5 February 1989.

[20] Martin Smith, *Burma* (London: Zed Press, 1991), p. 28; Roy Pateman, *Eritrea* (Trenton, N.J.: Red Sea Press, 1990), p. 6.

[21] Smith, *Burma*, p. 98.

[22] Ibid., p. 10.

Whereas foreign involvement in Burma's wars has been negligible, the Soviet Union provided large quantities of military assistance to the Ethiopian regime to suppress the Eritrean rebellion in the north of Ethiopia. For their part, the Eritreans received some support from Arab states, but most of their weaponry was captured from the Ethiopian army.[23] These weapons escalated the casualties of some pitched battles between Ethiopians and Eritreans, reaching into the thousands.[24]

It is remarkable that so many geographically dispersed and culturally distinct revolutionary regimes have become embroiled in similar conflicts. Many of the interstate wars were between historical rivals, and ethnic conflicts often antedated not only revolution but even colonialism. Still, contemporary revolutions have provoked much conflict. While tension between the United States and the Soviet Union exacerbated many conflicts (as did the struggle over apartheid in South Africa), the origins of conflict remain, for the most part, squarely within the revolutionary process. Those who propelled the revolutions forward sometimes felt they had no recourse other than to embrace one of the "superpowers," but often they openly took the lead in the courtship of an alliance. More important, by clinging to a utopian model of social transformation alien to their societies, revolutionary elites engendered local resistance. That resistance was often shamelessly manipulated from outside, but at least part of the responsibility for the outcome must rest with the revolutionaries who opened Pandora's box.

Conclusion

It is hard to believe that revolutionary elites were fully prepared for the enormous strife and carnage that accompanied radical political and social change. Their public transcript suggests only hubris, bravado, and unbridled hostility to those who stood in the way of revolutionary initiatives. Typical is a passage from a speech by Samora Machel in Mozambique:

> We are going to destroy the enemy. The people are determined. They are the main strength. We shall not fight with toffees. . . . We shall take firm measures to smash counter-revolution. We shall cut off the limb infected with gangrene. We shall remove the enemy from within. We shall cut the

[23] Roy Pateman, *Eritrea*, pp. 117–55.
[24] Ibid., pp. 135–148.

umbilical cord that links him to the former master, with hatchet and axe if necessary. Usually you take a pair of scissors to cut the umbilical cord, don't you? In this case, it will be a hatchet or axe.[25]

Commonly, enemies of the revolution are not only dehumanized, but also stripped of their nationality, being portrayed as puppets of foreign conspiracies.

In the aftermath of the Sandinista electoral defeat in Nicaragua, though, Sergio Ramírez, who served as vice-president, wrote a moving testament that acknowledged the political and moral complexity of conflict accompanying revolution. Ramírez recounts his experience at a public ceremony in an isolated rural area:

> During the ceremony a peasant from Morrito was to hand over his rifle to me in public. He had been fighting for the counter-revolution but had laid down his arms a few days earlier. A gaunt, little man in poor clothes climbed on to the platform, looking just like a plucked bird. . . . This little man, cowed by the spectacle, dropped his rifle into my hands and vanished. What world existed inside his head? . . . Was my world different? Were the two worlds connected? . . . I was committed to providing that peasant and his family with a new way of life. . . . But, attempting to reorganize his life from our far-off centers of revolutionary power, we were imposing our ideas of freedom on him. . . . We were losing the peasants, and our plans for collectivized farming seriously undermined all possibility of winning them over to our project. . . . That is why the counter-revolutionary war gradually became a peasant war, dividing the peasants into those who understood the revolution, and those who could not be reached by it.[26]

Ramírez's honesty makes it easier to understand—and even to empathize with—conscripts on both sides of revolutionary wars. He also points an explanatory finger at, and assigns a moral burden to, those who were imposing their ideas from "far-off centers of revolutionary power."

[25] Barry Munslow, ed.; Michael Wolfers, trans., *Samora Machel* (London: Zed Books, 1985), p. 94.
[26] Sergio Ramírez, "Election Night in Nicaragua," *Granta* 36 (Summer 1991): 117–118.

7

The Withering Away of an Idea

In 1990, two years before they were overthrown, the leaders of the People's Democratic Party of Afghanistan renounced Marxism. A ranking member of the party, Farid Mazdak, explained its former politics as reflecting the pressures of "a time when Marxism-Leninism was quite in fashion in underdeveloped countries."[1] At roughly the same time, in far away southern Africa, the president of Angola cautioned his colleagues that to insist on a one-party Marxist-Leninist state "would be rowing against the tide."[2] These metaphors of "fashion" and "tide" are suggestive. Beginning perhaps with Chinese agricultural reforms in 1978 and continuing through to the collapse of the Soviet Union in 1991, there was a sweeping loss of faith throughout Latin America, the Middle East, Africa, and Asia in the promise of revolution and in the dominant revolutionary ideology—socialism.

The turning of the tide, to continue the metaphor, cannot be simply explained. A number of complementary factors came into play and converged. Disgruntled peasants and workers dragged their feet; counterrevolutionaries and secessionists bled state and society; under the leadership of forceful conservatives, the United States and the United Kingdom aggressively promoted liberal democracy and unrestrained markets; the sympathy of intellectuals, beginning in Western Europe and North America, dissipated; and, finally, "real, existing" socialist states in Eastern Europe and the Soviet Union unraveled. In some instances, revolutionary elites were forced out of power. More commonly, revolutionary ideals were just abandoned by their erstwhile proponents. What had seemed possible, or even inevitable, suddenly was judged untenable.

The rapidity with which faith in socialism evaporated suggests that change did not come from the systematic diffusion of information and an incremental "political learning" by elites. While the aforementioned trends were important, they were so in an indirect way: they undermined revolution and socialism as paradigms, and they fostered

---

[1] Quoted in Seymour Lipset, "No Third Way," in Daniel Chirot, ed., *The Crisis of Leninism and the Decline of the Left* (Seattle: University of Washington, 1991), p. 205.

[2] Arthur Banks, ed., *Political Handbook of the World* (Binghamton, N.Y.: CSA Publishers, 1991), p. 22.

successive paradigms—democracy and market economics. Until the visionary and energizing paradigms of revolution and socialism were replaced, unflattering reportage and commentary about socialism were shrugged off or ignored. It takes an idea to refute an idea. The substitution of a political paradigm, or of the dominant intellectual culture, explains not only the abruptness of change in revolutionary regimes but also the degree to which the change was embraced by countries with different geographical and cultural settings, and varying temporal histories of revolution, ranging from a single decade to three decades.

Ordinarily, the prosaic working of government does not induce profound, systemic reflection about the framework of ideas that beget institutions, policy goals, and instruments, or even about the nature of the problems that government should address. There are times, though, when the intellectual culture that sustains a prevailing framework is widely scrutinized. At these special—and rare—moments, politics is driven not only by contests for power, but by doubts and uncertainty and by collective speculation about what to do.

The accession of a political doctrine is explained in part through the way in which the ideas comprising the doctrine relate to immediate economic and political problems. Put somewhat differently, persuasiveness is determined as much by the shape of current circumstances as by the content and merit of the ideas themselves. But the interplay between ideas and circumstance is most intricate and difficult to divine. A precise explanation of why one political doctrine is replaced by another is always elusive. Still, it is illuminating to delineate the set of circumstances that contributed to the withering away of a particularly potent political imagination throughout the poorest parts of the world.

Challenges to the Socialist Paradigm

Contemporary revolutionary states have typically foreclosed open opposition and protest. Moreover, the formal bodies that purport to represent the interests of "the masses" are often only transmission belts for instructions from the authorities. But workers and peasants have an arsenal of everyday forms of resistance, such as foot-dragging and false compliance, with which to signal their disagreement with revolutionary initiatives. The potential consequences are suggested by James Scott:

> Over the long run, and frequently at tragic costs to themselves, people involved in everyday forms of resistance can provoke a fiscal crisis that leads

to a change in policy. The massive economic reforms implemented in the People's Republic of China beginning in 1978 . . . are a case in point. From one perspective, the dismantling of the collectives, the inauguration of the "family responsibility system," the encouragement of petty trade and markets, may be viewed as a rational, centrally made decision to encourage growth by far-reaching reforms. While such a view is not precisely wrong, it entirely misses the fact that the everyday forms of peasant resistance over nearly two decades were instrumental in forcing this massive policy change.[3]

Strategies employed included the underreporting of land and other assets; misreporting of production; filing of exaggerated claims about thefts, waste, and spoilage; illegal procurements; misuse of state property; hoarding; and the reallocation of time away from collective tasks and to private economic activities. The prosaic, self-serving acts of thousands of laborers and petty producers have deprived contemporary revolutionary regimes of the wherewithal to maintain their power and prevail against their enemies.

At the other end of the continuum from foot-dragging as a form of opposition to politically closed revolutionary regimes is open revolt. As detailed in the preceding chapter, many contemporary revolutionary regimes have become bogged down with wars, including civil wars, or ethnic secession movements. While threats to national sovereignty or "territorial integrity" are often used to drum up support for an embattled regime, armed conflict—or even the continuing threat of it—wears down revolutionary regimes. The decision in 1989 of the Front for the Liberation of Mozambique (FRELIMO) to abandon its commitment to Marxism-Leninism, and so to revolution, was an explicit effort to seek accommodation with the persistent Mozambique National Resistance (RENAMO) rebels. The Sandinistas agreed to hold elections in part to undermine U.S. support for the counterrevolution; Nicaraguans voted in 1990 to end the revolution in the belief that ousting the Sandinistas would bring peace. In the following year, the Ethiopian Revolution came to a close when Eritrean secessionists and Tigrean rebels (from the other prominent ethnic group in the north of Ethiopia) captured Addis Ababa, forcing the flight of Mengistu and his government.

Military challenges to revolutionary regimes were given a boost by the U.S. election in 1980 of Ronald Reagan. As part of a concerted effort to reestablish the international fortunes of the United States,

---

[3] James Scott, "Everyday Forms of Resistance," in Forrest Colburn, ed., *Everyday Forms of Peasant Resistance* (Armonk, N.Y.: M. E. Sharpe, 1989), pp. 15–16.

perceived to be declining, Reagan backed away from détente, raised defense expenditures, heated up anti-Soviet rhetoric, and attempted to "roll back communism" around the world. Efforts at the latter culminated in the "Reagan doctrine" of military assistance to anticommunist rebels in such countries as Nicaragua, Angola, and Afghanistan. In 1983, after a bloody quarrel within the leadership of the governing New Jewel Movement in Grenada, Reagan ordered an invasion by U.S. troops that abruptly ended Grenada's revolution.

While the Reagan administration's military assistance to anticommunist rebels posed an intractable burden to a number of revolutionary regimes, perhaps more significant was the extent of the administration's championing of democracy and "free markets," which fostered a competing paradigm to revolution and socialism in poor countries. The salience of Reagan's message was enhanced by the emergence of conservative leaders in Western Europe: Margaret Thatcher, Helmut Kohl, and even the nominally socialist François Mitterrand.

To a certain extent, Reagan's electoral victory in 1980 capped major changes in the climate of U.S. public opinion generally and in policy debates specifically. Americans were becoming critical of welfare-state politics, and they increasingly rejected the continued extension of federal government activity. Concurrently, there was a disturbing perception that the United States' position in the world was declining. The Soviet invasion of Afghanistan weakened the credibility of détente. The Iranian Revolution, and especially the seizure of the United States Embassy in Iran and its staff, generated embarrassment and hostility. Although President Carter had previously set in motion a drive for rearmament, the climate of foreign policy had changed, and Reagan effectively articulated that movement.[4]

This alteration in the climate of U.S. policies was voiced, and even shaped, by academics and politicians who questioned existing government policies. The intellectual questioning of the assumptions behind liberal domestic policies and détente was itself diverse, and generated a number of critics who could not readily be placed in any school or grouping.[5] In Western Europe, also, attacks by intellectuals on reigning orthodoxies found a receptive audience. For example, in Paris, young philosophers began to question Jean-Paul Sartre's famous pronouncement that Marxism was "the unsurpassable philosophy of our time." Brash but erudite assaults on the foundations of Marxism were made by such *nouveaux philosophes* as André Glucksmann and Ber-

---

[4] Gillian Peele, *Revival and Reaction* (Oxford: Clarendon Press, 1984), p. 170.
[5] Ibid., pp. 4–7.

nard-Henri Lóvy. Citing Aleksandr Solzhenitsyn's exposé of the Soviet prison system, they attacked French Marxists' refusal to acknowledge repression in Eastern Europe or to admit that oppression itself was the logical result—and not merely a Russian aberration—of Marxist-Leninist principles.

Criticisms of socialism had been made before, most prominently after the Soviet invasion of Hungary in 1956 and of Czechoslovakia in 1968. But for reasons that are elusive, the rhetoric of Ronald Reagan and Margaret Thatcher, the acerbic wit of U.S. neoconservatives, and the anti-Marxist assault in France were more readily welcomed in the 1980s. The bizarre fate of the two most prominent French Communist intellectuals was symbolic: Louis Althusser went insane and strangled his wife; Nicos Poulantzas committed suicide (leaping from a window, it is said, with his books in his arms). The larger consequences of this diffuse but very real surge in "conservatism" were disparate: they included an attack on both the welfare state and socialism. Repercussions were felt in both domestic and foreign policy. Casualties included everything from Keynesian economics, to Eurocommunism, to sympathy for revolutionary regimes in poor countries.

While it is necessary to be careful about inferring causal relationships, these political changes in the United States and Western Europe posed a challenge to the leadership of the Soviet Union:

> This is where the new political thinking began. American intransigence, Europeans' continued deference to Washington's strategic preferences, the eventual deployment of U.S. intermediate-range nuclear forces in Europe, the political and strategic costs of the Afghanistan intervention, and the continued existence of the anti-Soviet alignment of the world's major power centers were all international-political facts that did not set well with the expectations generated by the old thinking. The 1980–1985 experience of hunkering down in the face of what must have seemed to the Soviet leaders a cynical and hostile assault by the United States did not, of course, predetermine the demise of old thinking. But it led many experts to one or both of two conclusions: either the old model was wrong, or the Soviet Union was in decline. Neither reflected well on the Soviet leadership. Both played well with reformist sentiments among the elite.[6]

Within the Soviet Union itself, seemingly unsolvable economic problems presented another set of challenges to socialist theory.

Actually, there is evidence that, independently, the Soviet elite had already begun to be disillusioned with revolutionary regimes through-

---

[6] William Wohlforth, *The Elusive Balance* (Ithaca: Cornell University Press, 1993), p. 228.

out Latin America, the Middle East, Africa, and Asia. Skepticism in inner circles mounted in the 1970s, as evidence accumulated about the poor performance of these regimes and the seemingly low returns to Soviet involvement with them. With the ascension of Mikhail Gorbachev in 1985, these doubts, which had been multiplying, were publicly voiced.

> The struggle for the Third World, already heavily devalued during the . . . early 1980s, was now widely regarded as an absurd diversion from which the Soviet Union should withdraw as quickly as possible. . . . Third World "socialism" was a cloak for brutal dictatorships and a tactic for wheedling money out of an ideologically gullible Soviet Union.[7]

The Soviet leadership withdrew its troops from Afghanistan in 1989 and sponsored regional settlements in southern Africa and Cambodia. Subsidies to revolutionary regimes were reduced. These and similar policy decisions were made possible by what, in the Soviet Union, was called "new thinking."

Although there were economic and political reasons to retrench from "revolutionary militancy," a different interpretation of events was possible, as was a strategy of simply ignoring obstacles, trenchant as they might be. Given the centralized government of the Soviet Union, Gorbachev's role in articulating and promoting "new thinking" was decisive. And his appointment, or the appointment of someone else with similar convictions and will, was not inevitable.

When Eastern Europe began to stir politically, the Soviet Union, under Gorbachev's leadership, did not intervene. The remarkable sequence of events in Eastern Europe, from the Polish strikes in 1988 to the collapse of the Berlin Wall in November of 1989, would not have been possible without Soviet acquiescence. In turn, unanticipated outcomes in Eastern Europe further weakened the Soviets' belief in their ideology and institutions. Reforms designed in Moscow to shore up the Soviet Union, including the dismantling of collective agriculture, led to the collapse of the first socialist state—the largest country in the world. In December 1991, the Soviet Union was dissolved. By the time it happened, few were surprised.

For revolutionary regimes in the poorer parts of the world, the dissolution of the Soviet Union was a monumental event. For many regimes, from Cuba to Mozambique to Vietnam, the Soviet Union had been a major donor of desperately needed foreign assistance. Although this assistance was never bountiful, except perhaps in the case of Cuba, it ensured the survival of revolutionary regimes. Arguably

---

[7] Ibid., p. 274.

more important, though, the Soviet Union had served as a model. While the Soviet Union was not always the original source of inspiration for revolutionary change, as argued in Chapter 2, it was always necessary for political elites to be able to point to a successful, if distant, case of the implementation of their ideals. If, after seventy years of sacrifice in following the founding precepts of Lenin himself, the Soviet Union could not sustain its revolutionary initiatives, what hope could exist for the poorest countries of the world?

Beginning in the second half of the 1980s, many revolutionary elites tried to accommodate themselves to the loss of international patronage, to the shifting of intellectual paradigms, to the decline of faith in revolutionary transformations, and to a renewed belief in democracy and unfettered markets. The new paradigm was not embraced with enthusiasm, but instead grudgingly, half-heartedly, and, commonly, with a desire to protect accumulated political (if not economic) power. Somewhat paradoxically, given the bitterness of Africa's civil wars, it was on that continent that there was greatest initial willingness to embrace both political democracy and economic reforms, leading to the retrenchment of the state. In 1990, the People's Democratic Republic of Yemen surrendered its commitment to socialism by merging with the Yemen Arab Republic. Elsewhere, especially in Asia, the common response to the collapse of socialism was market reforms but tight political control by ensconced political elites who all but abandoned revolutionary iconography and phraseology. Despite lingering vestiges, an era ended.

In Vietnam, for example, the Vietnamese Communist Party adopted at its Sixth National Congress in 1986 a comprehensive reform program. Prominent was an acceleration of the "decollectivization" of agriculture. The reforms had a quick and significant effect: Vietnam reemerged in 1989 as a rice exporter after two decades of being a net importer of rice.[8] But as was common elsewhere, Vietnam's reforms also included a revamping of cultural discourse and practice, including gender relations. The socialist image of the Vietnamese woman was as worker, fighter, and mother, and there was strong disapproval of the image of woman as sex object. In contrast is the 1989 Miss Ho Chi Minh City bathing-beauty contest (in which all contestants were examined by doctors to make sure that they were virgins).[9] These kinds of changes in social values suggest that the well-publicized

[8] Prabhu Pingali and Vo-Tong Xuan, "Vietnam," *Economic Development and Cultural Change* 40 (July 1992): 697.

[9] Kristin Pelzer, "Socio-Cultural Dimensions of Renovation in Vietnam," in William Turley and Mark Selden, eds., *Reinventing Vietnamese Socialism* (Boulder, Colo.: Westview Press, 1993), p. 319.

economic "reforms" are only part of a much wider change in governing paradigms.

In the one contemporary revolutionary case where socialism did not
provide the dominant inspiration—in Iran—religious fervor seems to
be burning itself out. Pragmatism and toleration increasingly replace
piety, foreshadowing what Crane Brinton called the Thermidor, a period of convalescence from revolution's inevitable reign of terror and
virtue. For example, constraints grounded in Islam that require Iranian
women to cover all but their faces and hands appear to be fading.[10]
Black marketeers, no longer fearful of public flogging, have flooded
markets with banned United States videos and cassette tapes, and with
cheap copies of Western European handbags, blouses, and scarfs.[11]
Fewer cabinet ministers are clerics. Economic criteria have become
more pronounced in the allocation of state resources. In evading the
lure of Marxism-Leninism, the Iranian Revolution was the most original of contemporary revolutions. Yet its religious zeal has been difficult to sustain in Iran itself, and it will not likely serve as a source of
renewed inspiration for revolution in other poor countries.

The discrediting of a generation of revolutionary ideology leaves
for the moment a vacuum. Will there be a new formulation of utopia?
If so, what will it be? To what extent will it propel political actors? A
veil of mystery now surrounds those interrogations. We are not at the
end of history, but doubtless at a moment of a new and uncertain
beginning.

[10] *New York Times*, 11 June 1991.
[11] *New York Times*, 12 April 1992.

8

Conceptual and Theoretical Considerations

I REMEMBER WALKING through Addis Ababa's huge central plaza during the country's relentless pursuit of socialism. Although it was often empty, it seemed the center of Addis Ababa, and so perhaps of Ethiopia itself. Ethiopia is one of the oldest countries of the world, given its name by the ancient Greeks. It is the only country in Africa that was never colonized by the voracious Europeans. Yet in the aftermath of the Ethiopian Revolution—which ended imperial rule—Addis Ababa's central plaza, renamed Revolutionary Square, was dominated by an enormous billboard bearing the portraits of three Europeans: Marx, Engels, and Lenin. As I strolled past majestic Coptic priests in flowing robes, I wondered if it occurred to them that the Ethiopia which had resisted European encroachment for generations was exalting and following dissident and now discredited Europeans. How could they not notice, I wondered too, that the tallest statue in the city commemorated not one of the many heroes in the Ethiopian pantheon, but a foreigner, a European—Lenin.

In the countryside, seemingly every village had a small billboard with the portraits of Marx, Engels, and Lenin. If the village was large, the billboard was in color; if the village was small, the billboard was black, gray, and white. What did the peasants think of these portraits? Did they wonder where they had come from? Did they wonder why their lives should be so brutally disrupted by adherence to the philosophy of these three foreigners?

For intellectuals and the young, educated military officers who together formed the leadership of the Ethiopian Revolution, socialism was a way to battle feudalism, neocolonialism, capitalism, and economic and political dependence on Europe and the United States. Socialism was propagated because of the increased opportunities for higher education made possible by Haile Selassie's regime in the aftermath of the Second World War. European political and social ideas amorphously and anonymously entered the country and came to exert a tremendous influence. These ideas greatly intensified the impatience of urban Ethiopians with their country's backwardness and antiquated government. In a less defined manner, these imported ideas redressed individual desires for dignity and the assertion of equality, numbed by feelings of inferiority vis-à-vis European wealth and influence.

The precepts of Marxism-Leninism appeared to explain the contradiction between inspiring European political concepts of liberty and equality and hated European practices of imperialism. Few students or military officers had much property or any vested interest in capitalism, so they had no reason to be frightened by the socialist economics of Marxism. And since imperialism (or colonialism or neocolonialism) was equated with capitalism, hostility to European and United States intrusions into Africa quite naturally stoked hostility to capitalism.

The attitudes and thinking of these privileged Ethiopians were typical of an entire generation of young, urban, educated men and women throughout most of those parts of the world overrun by European colonialism. This is not to suggest that every young individual with the opportunity to read and study became radicalized; nor is it to suggest that radicals everywhere believed in exactly the same things. But perhaps for the first time ever, a shared educational experience in Europe and the United States by a generation of talented and justifiably disaffected individuals made it possible for a relatively common intellectual culture to arise throughout the poorer countries of the world, from Latin America, to the Middle East, to Africa, and to Asia. Ironically, that intellectual culture was spawned by Europe and the United States, which continued to mediate and swell the flow of ideas and information.

After 1945, in the aftermath of the world's most destructive war, waged ironically by those countries that claimed the mantle of civilization, those throughout the poorer parts of the world with the luxury of having a political imagination came to share a set of political views, based overwhelmingly on the writings of European dissidents and dreamers: Marx, Engels, and Lenin. But it was not a coherent ideology. Instead, it was mysticism of an almost religious character, which lent not only a methodology for understanding, criticizing, and imagining social structures, political institutions, and economic systems, but also an attitude of self-righteous militancy. This in-vogue *mentalité*, or political imagination, was infused with a fluid ensemble of images and concepts, obscure and replete with unconscious elements. Sometimes the outcome of such beliefs was political intoxication, which could alternatively be inspiring or frightful.

As it was being locally appropriated, this *mentalité* was most likely fused not with other kinds of political thinking (such as liberalism), but instead with religions: with Confucianism, with Buddhism, with Islam, and with Christianity. Buddhism mediated the adoption of socialism in Burma, while Christianity tempered socialism in Nicaragua. Only Islam has proved a match for socialism. The embrace of socialism by students and intellectuals in Afghanistan and South Yemen added impetus to the clerical movement. In Egypt, Indonesia, and Iran, socialism and Islam appear to have concurrently filled an intellectual vacuum. While sharing an aversion to the political and economic reach of Europe and the United States, the two doctrines have had an explosive interaction throughout the Islamic world.

Ideas alone do not explain contemporary revolutions. Indisputably, the many revolutions between 1945 and 1990 in poor countries were facilitated by the decline of colonialism that began with the Second World War. And sundry dictatorships were bound to collapse sooner or later, leaving easy picking to revolutionary challengers and their successors. How long, for example, could Ethiopia continue to be governed by an emperor? Structural variables such as the economy, class stratification, state strength, and international forces certainly are important for an understanding of the course and configuration of contemporary revolutions. Political and economic structures help explain why certain regimes were vulnerable, both because they were ineffectual in solving problems and because they did not enjoy legitimacy, while other regimes were not vulnerable—even in the face of aggressive proponents of radical change.

The argument of this work is much more than that a popular and powerful political idea helped push tottering regimes over the edge of a precipice. The power of such ideas is real and deserves appreciation. A more central concern is the extent to which the vogue of socialism, despite vagaries in its comprehension, served to shape revolutionary politics. Revolution brings the moment of supreme political choice. To an extent otherwise never possible, it can be asked: How should we be governed, and to what ends shall our government propel us? Persuasively, socialism provided answers. But the socialist cast to the remaking of political discourse and of government institutions and policies was neither foreordained nor historically inevitable.

Intellectual fashion led many leaders in the poorer countries of the world simply to mouth the slogans of socialism and to champion its cause in their speeches. Often this rhetoric was little more than political theater, useful for neutralizing the appeal of committed socialists and for capturing the approval of an ill-informed public. Socialist rhetoric could sometimes mask authoritarian, personal rule and project a "progressive" regional image. The idea of revolutionary socialism could thus be employed profitably without requiring any political "hard choices" (defined as those choices with a cost or at least a trade-off) domestically or internationally.[1]

[1] Kenneth Jowitt, "Scientific Socialist Regimes in Africa," in Carl Rosberg and Thomas Callaghy, eds., *Socialism in Sub-Sahara Africa* (Institute of International Studies, University of California, Berkeley, 1979), p. 135.

Yet in many countries, revolution and socialism meant more than fashionable phraseology and iconography. It is difficult to distinguish which political movements and efforts at political change were truly revolutionary. This study has identified twenty-two regime changes between 1945 and 1990 that can be considered revolutionary, all of them in the poorer countries of the world. Whether or not one wishes to add or subtract from the list, it remains remarkable how many impoverished countries were led for a time by political elites who believed that they had the wherewithal to remake radically their countries. And in these cases, dominant ideas about revolution and socialism influenced the hard choices of government: the kinds of political institutions to be constructed, the political processes to be promoted, the level of social mobilization to be attained, the organization of the economy, the international alliances, and the setting of goals for the polity.

Revolutions will always be monumental undertakings; the seeking to implement socialist beliefs made them even more Herculean. Mao asserted in 1958, "Ours is an ardent nation, now swept by a burning tide. There is a good metaphor for this: our nation is like an atom. . . . When this atom's nucleus is smashed the thermal energy released will have really tremendous power. We shall be able to do things which we could not do before."[2] All of the formidable resources that regimes could muster—including real and threatened coercion—were marshaled to submit their populace to an inspirational ideological construct with little specifity and with no evidence of its applicability.

With temporal and geographical distances, it is hard to recapture the abundant sense of possibility, the hopefulness, and the fervent passion of those who were enthralled with revolution. The following two poems offer a glimmer of insight. The first is from China:

> Everyone eats full without pay
> Our ancestors never heard of it!
> Is it a dream?
> No, it's a fact!
> Where?
> Right here!
> The East is red! Hail to Mao Zedong![3]

More extraordinary, perhaps, is the following contemporary poem from Ethiopia, where conversion to Christianity took place in the fourth century. The poem is titled, "The Trinity."

---

[2] Quoted in Stuart Schram, ed.; John Chinnery and Tieyun, trans., *Chairman Mao Talks to the People* (New York: Pantheon Books, 1974), p. 33.

[3] Ranbir Vohra, *China* (New Delhi: Penguin, 1990), p. 56.

The myth of the old book
  Reveals in the New Book.
Three in Flesh
  But One in Soul.
Three in One
  And One in Three.
The Trinity in Unity
  For Man's Liberty!
Marx the Father
  Engels the Son
And Lenin
  The Holy Ghost
Made the new Man
  Free from slavery![4]

The author of the poem also penned the "National Anthem of Socialist Ethiopia."

These poems reflect the exuberance that was ushered in by revolution. However, it was the deeds inspired by the new political imagination that were most consequential. Some revolutionary policies have born fruit, including often reduced inequality, heightened literacy, and broader access to health services. For the most part, though, socialist revolutionary initiatives have failed. The ideas, however inspiring by themselves, did not prevail when confronted with the social and material realities of the world's poorer countries.

There have been many tragedies, too. China's Great Leap Forward, perhaps symbolic of the era's revolutionary experience, aggravated a famine that resulted in the death of an estimated twenty million Chinese. And China's subsequent Cultural Revolution resulted in widespread disruption, deprivation, and death. Impractical agrarian policies exacerbated a famine in Ethiopia that killed a million Ethiopians; the deaths of another eight million were averted only with massive foreign aid. Hundreds of thousands of Iranian boys and young men were sent to certain martyrdom shouting "God is great!" in the country's war with Iraq. Contentious politics in Angola and Mozambique led to civil wars that devastated the infrastructure and led to the deaths of perhaps half a million Africans. A hasty revolution in Afghanistan led to a civil war in which a million Afghans lost their lives. Draconian social and economic policies in Cambodia led to the death of roughly an eighth of the population—another million deaths for the frenzied pursuit of a dreamt-up world. Behind these national tragedies are countless smaller tragedies, of families and of individuals. The

[4] Assefa Gmt, *The Voice* (Addis Ababa: Chamber Printing House, 1980), p. 33.

mostly unrecorded stories are of diaspora, unremunerated toil, priva-
tion, and the squandering of hope.

Revolutions are always messy and bloody. But the contemporary
revolutions in the poorer countries of the world seem especially costly.
That excessive cost, worsened by the paltriness of the benefits, can be
traced to a noble but sadly flawed political imagination that provided
inspiration and guidance to the revolutionaries. It was a paradigm that
did not emerge from the realities of the poor countries of Latin America, the Middle East, Africa, and Asia; and it did not fit those realities.

These are my sober conclusions. There is no shortage of scholarly
work pointing out the peculiarities of individual cases of contemporary revolution. They are useful works. Here, I have tried to show how
recent revolutions have demonstrated some commonality, even in
their diversity. My analysis differs, too, in that rather than look for
structurally determined origins and outcomes, I have tried to elucidate
the sources of convergence and divergence in revolutionary politics.
Innovations in the forms and meanings of politics were not predetermined, accidental, or inconsequential.

The politics of revolution is taken seriously by examining the ways
in which ideas, rhetoric, symbols, and the participation of certain
groups decisively influenced revolutionary change. Departing from
the two most prominent paradigms of Marxism and modernization, I
have concentrated on the unfolding of the revolutionary event. An understanding of revolutionary politics is important for theorizing about
revolutions, because in the geographically and culturally diverse
poorer countries of the world, the commonality and coherence of revolution comes from the shared values and political imagination of political elites.

In pointing to the power of ideas in explaining contemporary revolutions, I reject the notion that at any given moment all ideas are
equally visible, compelling, and accessible. This perspective deprecates
the influence of ideas and instead posits that political actors are forced
by some magnetlike "structural" or institutional variable to adopt a
given idea from a neutral arena. There are fashions in ideas as well as
in clothes, and revolution was one. Ideological fashion surely has a
"material base," but this is incomplete in its sway. Fashion can take on
its own momentum, its own inexplicable quirks and deviations. Just as
important, fashion can exact an imperfect but still surprising confor-
mity where none would otherwise exist.

There are three advantages to viewing revolution as more than an
opera between long-term causes and effects. First, it questions the opti-
mism of both Marxism and modernization theory, which had assumed
that revolutions, no matter how chaotic, somehow lead to a lurching

ahead to a more efficient social organization of the "means of production" or to a "resynchronization" of formerly "dysfunctional societies." Revolutions are not necessarily the "locomotives of history" or crucibles of modernity. Depending on revolutionary politics, societies may lurch forward, fall backward, stagger, or even implode. Likewise, states do not invariably become more centralized or stronger. The initial conclusions by many scholars, that contemporary revolutions were creating stronger states and a heightened sense of nationhood, seem now quite premature—and often just plain wrong—as trenchant economic problems and a diminution of social legitimacy have exposed and exacerbated the weaknesses of many revolutionary regimes.

Second, if the ideas, rhetoric, symbols, and forms of political activity of revolutionary participants matter, then it becomes possible to consider the fact that there are choices. Ideas can differ, rise, and fall in fashion, and so political behavior can correspondingly vary. With choice comes the possibility of different outcomes. Thus, for example, the liberalism of the French Revolution proved politically durable. And it is even possible to have revolutions that are not propelled by a novel political imagination. Indeed, as the French historian François Furet remarked, "With all the fuss and noise, not a single new idea . . . [came] out of Eastern Europe in 1989."[5]

The trajectory of contemporary revolutionary regimes illuminates why, at least in poor countries, the choices of political elites are so consequential. In many such countries, political elites are not significantly constrained by either the institutions and norms of government or by civil society. Thus, the time for experimentation and implementation of ideas can be dangerously compressed. In these settings, dazzling ideas can be most pernicious, most likely to overcome rationality.

Heeding revolutionary politics is also important because it decidedly lessens the danger of reification so common in the sweeping structural analyses of Marxist and modernization theorists, in which often no one is responsible for anything. How the lives of millions of people were touched by revolution deserves to be a focus of scholarship, as much as does the generation of parsimonious theories of historical change. Both narratives and analyses of revolution should be infused with the vividness necessary to discern the effects of idealism and tragedy. A greater appreciation for the role of politics is more likely to raise, too, the hitherto neglected question of moral responsibility, as "sweeping historical forces" are replaced by choices made by individuals or groups. If political actors are regarded as morally

[5] Quoted in Ralf Dahrendorf, *Reflections on the Revolution in Europe* (New York: Times Books, 1990), p. 27.

responsible individuals, rather than as products of impersonal historical forces, then the quality of their stewardship is a matter that scholars should be more prepared to observe, analyze, and even judge.

Within the heterogeneous field of the study of politics, some scholars eschew structural analyses in favor of a choice-centered approach.
These scholars frequently employ the methodology of microeconomic
analysis to explain how the rational behavior of individuals or groups
creates unexpected political outcomes. Alternatively, the independent
and dependent variables are reversed: perplexing political behavior is
explained by means of the rational behavior of interested parties.
Scholars working within this tradition have not attempted to analyze
the totality of revolutions, as have those working within the Marxist
and modernization paradigms. However, they have, on occasion,
sought to explain important components of revolution. For example,
fruitful studies have examined revolutionary strategy, the behavior of
managers of nationalized enterprises, and peasant resistance to agrarian policies.[6]

Invariably, though, these studies take either the pursuit or the existence of a revolution as a given. Revolution appears only as a prominent feature of the "strategic context" within which actors make
choices, imposing constraints on self-interested behavior.[7] Yet, for a
satisfactory understanding of revolution, the revolutionary impulse itself has to be explained, and only the most reductionist theorist would
argue that the radical urge to remake state and society is either completely "rational" or "self-interested."[8]

Put another way, this approach can perhaps explain the behavior of
a Cuban bureaucrat or peasant, but it is at a loss to explain Fidel Castro. His leadership of the Cuban Revolution cannot be explained solely
as a result of changes in objective conditions or material interests. His
ideas—and he is full of them—are consequential because they surely
shape his decisions. Explaining revolutionary elites' ideas is crucial,
because in a revolution ideas are more than a kind of intervening variable that mediates interests and outcomes. Ideas transform perceptions of interests, sometimes wildly so. They shape actors' perceptions
of possibilities, as well as their understanding of their interests.

---

[6] See, for example, James DeNardo, *Power in Numbers* (Princeton: Princeton University Press, 1985).

[7] Kathleen Thelen and Sven Steinmo, "Historical Institutionalism in Comparative Politics," in Sven Steinmo, et al., eds., *Structuring Politics* (Cambridge: Cambridge University Press, 1992), p. 7.

[8] In the lexicon of economic analysis, revealed preferences have to be explained, a
difficult research endeavor with only the methodology of economics available.

A complete understanding of revolution necessarily leads one into the murky world of passion and imagination. At some point, the confounding question needs to be broached: What is the origin of ideas, of understood possibilities? It is difficult to maintain analytical rigor because, in the end, revolution is neither predictable nor rational. Indeed, no revolution is ever really "necessary." There are no sufficient causes. The century's greatest revolutionary stressed the contingency of the Russian Revolution. In a remarkable passage, Lenin said:

> If the Revolution has triumphed so rapidly it is exclusively because, as a result of a historical situation of extreme originality, a number of completely distinct currents, a number of totally heterogeneous class interests, and a number of completely opposite social and political tendencies have become fused with remarkable coherence.[9]

In the course of producing the highly improbable event of revolution, passion and imagination are crucial, through the formation and sustenance of demonizations, sanctifications, and, above all, aspirations.

Revolution defies not just established political and economic realities, but also the petty calculations of interest and advantage that comprise so much of everyday life. The prosaic is set aside. In describing Pol Pot, a former companion of his appropriated the celebrated remark by the Russian revolutionary Axelrod about Lenin: that he was "the only man who had no thoughts but thoughts about the revolution, and who in his sleep dreamt of revolution."[10] Other revolutionary leaders who followed Lenin in this century, drawn from some of the poorest countries of the world, were similarly politically intoxicated by revolution during the epoch it was in vogue.

[9] Quoted in Albert Hirschman, "The Search for Paradigms as a Hinderance to Understanding," *World Politics* 22 (April 1970): 342.

[10] Henry Kamm, "Sowing the Killing Fields," *New York Times Book Review*, 12 January 1992: 7.

PLATES

Anniversary of the October Revolution. Lenin and Neto Have the Same
Objective: Socialism. Angola, poster, 1978–1979.

First National Agricultural Seminar, 1975. Mozambique, poster, 1975.

May 1—International Worker's Day. Mozambique, poster, 1970s.

Medal. Ethiopia, collected in Asmara, 1987.

Military parading at Revolutionary Square in front of a billboard portraying
Marx, Engels, and Lenin. Ethiopia, postcard, 1980s.

Mao with a cigar. China, magazine cover, 1967.

Oil workers receiving their copies of the quotations of Mao. China, magazine illustration, 1971.

Ho Chi Minh with soldiers. Vietnam, magazine illustration, 1968.

Female soldier. Vietnam, magazine illustration, 1968.

Guardian (female soldier). Burma, magazine cover, 1989.

Fidel Castro. Cuba, cover of training manual, 1960.

Entering Havana on 8 January 1959. Cuba, obverse of a one-peso currency note, 1980.

Guerrilla firing a gun from the cover of a barricade. Nicaragua, from the masthead of the Sandinista newspaper, *Barricada*, 1979.

The Militia in Action. Nicaragua, magazine cover, circa 1983.

Poster. Grenada, circa 1980.

Bibliography

Amirahmadi, Hooshang. *Revolution and Economic Transition*. Albany: State University of New York Press, 1990.

Amjad, Mohammed. *Iran*. Westport, Conn.: Greenwood Press, 1989.

Anwar, Raja. *The Tragedy of Afghanistan*, translated by Khalid Hasan. London: Verso, 1988.

Appleby, Joyce. *Liberalism and Republicanism in the Historical Imagination*. Cambridge: Harvard University Press, 1992.

Ascher, William. *Scheming for the Poor*. Cambridge: Harvard University Press, 1984.

Assefa Gmt. *The Voice*. Addis Ababa: Chamber Printing House, 1980.

Bakhash, Shaul. *The Reign of the Ayatollahs*, rev. ed. New York: Basic Books, 1990.

Banks, Arthur, ed. *Political Handbook of the World*. Binghamton, N.Y.: CSA Publications, 1991.

Benjamin, Medea. "Things Fall Apart." *NACLA* 24 (August 1990): 13–22.

Berman, Paul. "Nicaragua 1986." *Mother Jones* (December 1990): 20–27 and 53–54.

Bishop, Maurice, and Chris Searle. *Grenada*. London: Education Committee for the British-Grenadian Friendship Society, 1981.

Brinton, Crane. *The Anatomy of Revolution*. New York: W. W. Norton, 1938.

Cabezas, Omar. *La montaña es algo más que una inmensa estepa verde*. Havana: Casa de las Américas, 1982.

Carmona, Fernando, ed. *Nicaragua*. Mexico City: Editorial Nuestro Tiempo, 1980.

Carr, E. H. *The Bolshevik Revolution*. Harmondsworth, Middlesex (England): Penguin, 1966.

Chandler, David. *The Tragedy of Cambodian History*. New Haven: Yale University Press, 1991.

Chang Pao-Min. *Kampuchea between China and Vietnam*. Kent Ridge: Singapore University Press, 1985.

Chartier, Roger. *The Cultural Origins of the French Revolution*, translated by Lydia Cochrane. Durham: Duke University Press, 1991.

Chen, King. *China's War with Vietnam, 1979*. Stanford: Hoover Institution Press, 1987.

Chilcote, Ronald. *Almícar Cabral*. Boulder, Colo.: Lynne Rienner, 1991.

Chubin, Shahram, and Charles Tripp. *Iran and Iraq at War*. London: I. B. Tauris, 1988.

Clapham, Christopher. *Transformation and Continuity in Revolutionary Ethiopia*. Cambridge: Cambridge University Press, 1988.

Colburn, Forrest. "Foot Dragging and Other Peasant Responses to the Nicaraguan Revolution." In *Everyday Forms of Peasant Resistance*, edited by Forrest Colburn, pp. 175–197. Armonk, N.Y.: M. E. Sharpe, 1989.

Colburn, Forrest. *Managing the Commanding Heights*. Berkeley: University of California Press, 1990.

———. *Post-Revolutionary Nicaragua*. Berkeley: University of California Press, 1986.

Crow, Ben, and Alan Thomas. *Third World Atlas*. Milton Keynes (England): Open University, 1983.

Dahrendorf, Ralf. *Reflections of the Revolution in Europe*. New York: Times Books, 1990.

Davidson, Basil. *The Liberation of Guiné*. Harmondsworth, Middlesex (England): Penguin, 1969.

Davies, James. "Toward a Theory of Revolution." *American Sociological Review* 27 (February 1962): 5–19.

Dawit Wolde Giorgis. *Red Tears*. Trenton, N.J.: Red Sea Press, 1989.

DeNardo, James. *Power in Numbers*. Princeton: Princeton University Press, 1985.

Dessalegn Rahmato. *Cabral and the Problem of the African Revolution*. Addis Ababa: Institute of Development Research, 1982.

Dix, Robert. "Why Revolutions Succeed and Fail." *Polity* 16 (Spring 1984): 423–446.

Duiker, William. *China and Vietnam*. Institute of East Asian Studies, University of California, Berkeley, 1986.

Dunn, John. *Modern Revolutions*, 2d ed. Cambridge: Cambridge University Press, 1989.

Eckstein, Harry. "On the Etiology of Internal Wars." *History and Theory* 4 (1965): 133–163.

Edwards, Lyford. *The Natural History of Revolution*. Chicago: University of Chicago Press, 1927.

Evans, Grant. *Lao Peasants under Socialism*. New Haven: Yale University Press, 1990.

Fairbank, John. *The Great Chinese Revolution*. New York: Harper & Row, 1986.

Franqui, Carlos. *Family Portrait with Fidel*, translated by Alfred MacAdam. London: Jonathan Cape, 1980.

Gall, Norman. "The Legacy of Che Guevara." *Commentary* 44 (December 1967): 31–44.

Galli, Rosemary, and Jocelyn Jones. *Guinea-Bissau*. London: Frances Pinter, 1987.

Goldstone, Jack. "Theories of Revolutions." *World Politics* 32 (April 1980): 425–453.

Gómez, Walter. "Bolivia." *Journal of Developing Areas* 10 (July 1976): 461–483.

Gorman, Stephen. "Power and Consolidation in the Nicaraguan Revolution." *Journal of Latin American Studies* 13 (May 1981): 133–149.

Granma Weekly Review, 14 December 1986.

Grevemeyer, Jan-Heeren. "Modernization from Below." In *The Tragedy of Afghanistan*, edited by Bol Huldt and Erland Jansson, pp. 121–147. London: Croom Helm, 1988.

Gurr, Ted. *Why Men Rebel*. Princeton: Princeton University Press, 1970.

Halliday, Fred. *Revolution and Foreign Policy*. Cambridge: Cambridge University Press, 1990.

Hanlon, Joseph. *Mozambique.* London: Zed Press, 1984.

Hirschman, Albert. "The Search for Paradigms as a Hindrance to Understanding." *World Politics* 22 (April 1970): 329–343.

Hook, Sidney. *The Hero in History.* New York: John Day, 1943.

Hopwood, Derek. *Egypt.* 3d ed. London: HarperCollins, 1991.

Humbaraci, Arslan. *Algeria.* New York: Praeger, 1966.

Hunt, Lynn. *Politics, Culture, and Class in the French Revolution.* Berkeley: University of California Press, 1984.

Huntington, Samuel. *Political Order in Changing Societies.* New Haven: Yale University Press, 1968.

Isaacman, Allen, and Barbara Isaacman. *Mozambique.* Boulder, Colo.: Westview Press, 1983.

Jackson, Karl. "The Ideology of Total Revolution." In *Cambodia 1975–1978*, edited by Karl Jackson, pp. 37–78. Princeton: Princeton University Press, 1989.

Johnson, Chalmers. *Revolutionary Change.* Boston: Little, Brown, 1966.

Jowitt, Kenneth. "Scientific Socialist Regimes in Africa." In *Socialism in Sub-Sahara Africa*, edited by Carl Rosberg and Thomas Callaghy, pp. 133–173. Institute of International Studies, University of California, Berkeley, 1979.

Judson, C. Fred. *Cuba and the Revolutionary Myth.* Boulder, Colo.: Westview Press, 1984.

Kahin, George. *Nationalism and Revolution in Indonesia.* Ithaca: Cornell University Press, 1952.

Kahin, George, and John Lewis. *The United States in Vietnam.* New York: Dell Publishing, 1967.

Kamm, Henry. "Sowing the Killing Fields." *New York Times Book Review*, 12 January 1992: 7.

Kamrava, Mehran. *Revolutionary Politics.* Westport, Conn.: Praeger, 1992.

Karnow, Stanley. "Giap Remembers." *New York Times Magazine*, 24 June 1990: 22–23, 36, 39, 57, 59–60, 62.

Keller, Edmond. *Revolutionary Ethiopia.* Bloomington: Indiana University Press, 1988.

Lewis, Gordon. *Grenada.* Baltimore: Johns Hopkins University Press, 1987.

Lipset, Seymour. "No Third Way." In *The Crisis of Leninism and the Decline of the Left*, edited by Daniel Chirot, pp. 183–232. Seattle: University of Washington Press, 1991.

Llerena, Mario. *The Unsuspected Revolution.* Ithaca: Cornell University Press, 1978.

Lopes, Carlos. *Guinea-Bissau.* Boulder, Colo.: Westview Press, 1987.

Malloy, James. "Generation of Political Support and Allocation of Costs." In *Revolutionary Change in Cuba*, edited by Carmelo Mesa-Lago, pp. 23–42. Pittsburgh: University of Pittsburgh Press, 1971.

Mandle, Jay. *Big Revolution, Small Country.* Lanham, Md.: North-South Publishing, 1985.

Marcum, John. "The People's Republic of Angola." In *Afro-Marxist Regimes*, edited by Edmond Keller and Donald Rothchild, pp. 67–83. Boulder, Colo.: Lynne Rienner, 1987.

Mathur, Girish. *New Afghanistan.* New Delhi: Sterling Publishers, 1983.

McVey, Ruth. *The Rise of Indonesian Communism*. Ithaca: Cornell University Press, 1965.

Mesa-Lago, Carmelo. *The Economy of Socialist Cuba*. Albuquerque: University of New Mexico Press, 1981.

Ministry of State Farms Development (Ethiopia). Untitled Report. Addis Ababa, 1985. Mimeographed.

Mondlane, Eduardo. *The Struggle for Mozambique*. Harmondsworth, Middlesex (England): Penguin, 1969.

Moore, Barrington, Jr. *Social Origins of Dictatorship and Democracy*. Boston: Beacon Press, 1966.

Morawetz, David. "Economic Lessons for Some Small Socialist Developing Countries." *World Development* 8 (May-June 1980): 337–369.

Munslow, Barry, ed.; Michael Wolfers, trans. *Samora Machel*. London: Zed Books, 1985.

Myerson, Michael. *Memories of Underdevelopment*. New York: Grossman, 1973.

Naipaul, V. S. "Argentina." *New York Review of Books* 39 (30 January 1992): 13–18.

New York Times.

Nolan, David. *The Ideology of the Sandinistas and the Nicaraguan Revolution*. Graduate School of International Studies, University of Miami, Coral Gables, 1984.

Ortega, Humberto. *50 años de lucha sandinista*. Mexico City: Editorial Diogenes, 1979.

Paige, Jeffrey. *Agrarian Revolution*. New York: Free Press, 1975.

Pateman, Roy. *Eritrea*. Trenton, N.J.: Red Sea Press, 1990.

Peele, Gillian. *Revival and Reaction*. Oxford: Clarendon Press, 1984.

Pelzer, Kristin. "Socio-Cultural Dimensions of Renovation in Vietnam." In *Reinventing Vietnamese Socialism*, edited by William Turley and Mark Selden, pp. 309–336. Boulder, Colo.: Westview Press, 1993.

Pettee, George. *The Process of Revolution*. New York: Harper, 1938.

Pingali, Prabhu, and Vo-Tong Xuan. "Vietnam." *Economic Development and Cultural Change* 40 (July 1992): 697–718.

Pryor, Frederic. *The Red and the Green*. Princeton: Princeton University Press, 1992.

Ramírez, Sergio. "Election Night in Nicaragua." *Granta* 36 (Summer 1991): 109–130.

Randall, Margaret. *Somos millones*. Mexico City: Editorial Extemporáneos, 1977.

Rock, David. *Argentina*. Berkeley: University of California Press, 1985.

Rodríguez, Carlos Rafael. *Letra con filo*, vol. 2. Havana: Editorial de Ciencias Sociales, 1983.

Rubinstein, Alvin. *Moscow's Third World Strategy*. Princeton: Princeton University Press, 1988.

Schram, Stuart, ed. John Chinnery and Tieyun, trans. *Chairman Mao Talks to the People*. New York: Pantheon Books, 1974.

———. *Mao Zedong*. Hong Kong: Chinese University Press, 1983.

Schurman, Franz. *Ideology and Organization in Communist China*, rev. ed. Berkeley: University of California Press, 1966.

Scott, James. "Everyday Forms of Resistance." In *Everyday Forms of Peasant Resistance*, edited by Forrest Colburn, pp. 3–33. Armonk, N.Y.: M. E. Sharpe, 1989.

———. *Weapons of the Weak*. New Haven: Yale University Press, 1985.

Seabury, Paul, and Walter McDougall, eds. *The Grenada Papers*. San Francisco: Institute for Contemporary Studies, 1984.

Shu, Austin. *On Mao Tse-Tung*. Asian Studies Center, Michigan State University, East Lansing, 1972.

Skocpol, Theda. *States and Social Revolutions*. Cambridge: Cambridge University Press, 1979.

Smelser, Neil. *Theory of Collective Behavior*. New York: Free Press, 1963.

Smith, Martin. *Burma*. London: Zed Press, 1991.

Sorokin, Pitrim. *The Sociology of Revolution*. Philadelphia: J. B. Lippincott, 1925.

Souresrafil, Behrouz. *The Iran-Iraq War*. Plainview, N.Y.: Guinan, 1989.

Spence, Jonathan. *The Search for Modern China*. New York: W. W. Norton, 1990.

State Statistics Bureau (China). *Statistical Yearbook of PRC*. Beijing: State Statistics Bureau, 1991.

Stone, Lawrence. "Theories of Revolution." *World Politics* 18 (October 1965): 159–176.

Thelen, Kathleen, and Sven Steinmo. "Historical Institutionalism in Comparative Politics." In *Structuring Politics*, edited by Sven Steinmo, Kathleen Thelen, and Frank Longstreth, pp. 1–32. Cambridge: Cambridge University Press, 1992.

Tilly, Charles. "Revolutions and Collective Violence." In Fred Greenstein and Nelson Polsby, eds., *Handbook of Political Science*, Reading, Mass.: Addison-Wesley, 1975: 483–555.

Trimberger, Kay. *Revolutions from Above*. New Brunswick, N.J.: Transaction Books, 1978.

Vines, Alex. *Renamo*. Centre for Southern African Studies, University of York (England), 1991.

Vohra, Ranbir. *China*. New Delhi: Penguin, 1990.

Walt, Stephen. "Revolution and War." *World Politics* 44 (April 1992): 321–368.

Wickham-Crowley, Timothy. *Exploring Revolution*. Armonk, N.Y.: M. E. Sharpe, 1991.

Williams, Michael. *Vietnam at the Crossroads*. London: Pinter, 1992.

Wohlforth, William. *The Elusive Balance*. Ithaca: Cornell University Press, 1993.

Wolf, Eric. *Peasant Wars of the Twentieth Century*. New York: Harper & Row, 1969.

Womack, Brantly. *The Foundation of Mao Zedong's Political Thought 1917–1935*. Honolulu: University Press of Hawaii, 1982.

Wylie, Raymond. *The Emergence of Maoism*. Stanford: Stanford University Press, 1980.

Young, Crawford. *Ideology and Development in Africa*. New Haven: Yale University Press, 1982.

Index

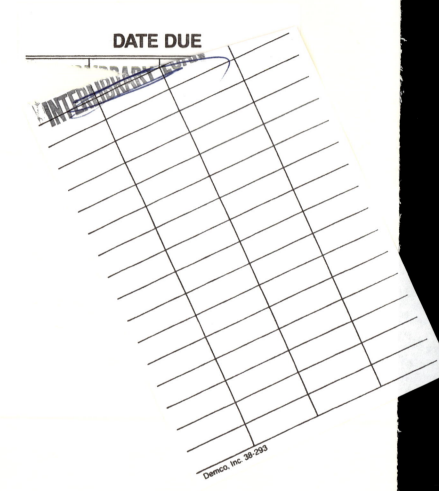